The Adaptive Toolkit for
Potty Training Children with Disabilities

Written by
Allison Jandu
The Potty Training Consultant

With Contributions by
Taryn Lagonigro & Jess Quarello
and the *Extra Lucky* Community

Four Clovers
PUBLISHING
Stories That Uplift, Empower, and Belong

A Four Clovers Publishing Publication
Four Clovers Publishing Registered Offices: Caldwell, NJ 07006
Copyright © 2024 by Allison Jandu, Taryn Lagonigro & Jessica Quarello

Library of Congress Control Number: 2024922904

Allison Jandu, Taryn Lagonigro & Jessica Quarello
The Adaptive Toolkit for Potty Training Children with Disabilities
ISBN: 979-8-9853136-6-6
Published in the United States of America

Book cover and inside design by Kristin Broek
Editing and creative design consultation by Elena Croy
Foreword by Lora Jackle
Photography by Carley Storm Branding Co
Graphics by Annalyce D'Agostino, Focus Posters

Table of Contents

This book is dedicated
to all the caregivers
in the disability community.
We know journeys like these
can feel overwhelming,
but by taking the first step,
you're already doing a great job.
You've got this.

Foreword

As a pediatric occupational therapist (OT) for the past 19 years, I have received **many** questions about potty training children of all abilities. Some of these questions I have been well-equipped to answer; pediatric OTs are considered the experts when it comes to self-help skills, and toileting is one of those basic activities of daily living covered from the very beginning of OT school. What many people do not understand, however, is just how many components there actually are to any activity we do, and using the potty is no exception! In a good OT program, from the very first class, students must complete "task/activity analysis" to truly understand this—breaking down a "simple" task to the most basic components and writing out every muscle action, body function, sensation, etc. that will be needed to complete the task. Therapy students quickly learn that a 60-second task (e.g., removing pants, getting onto the potty, and peeing on the potty) can easily become a 5-page paper when you break it down into each muscle function, nerve function, sensory system, internal and external communication, etc. What appears "simple" becomes very complex when you bring it down to a granular level, and the constant practice of analyzing everyday activities during the student years primes OTs to do this constantly while assessing and treating patients.

As an expert in task analysis and activities of daily living, I did not initially feel intimidated when it came to the concept of potty training my children. I had three children spread out over 14 years. With the first, though she did have some developmental disabilities and a complex medical diagnosis, I was young enough to be naïve, and luckily for 26-year-old me, things just sort of...worked out. We stumbled along together, figuring out what her little sensory system could tolerate and not, and though there were a few tears (mine, not hers), she achieved full potty-trained status within a few weeks. Eleven years later, along came her headstrong sister, and with more parenting experience I knew enough to have a little anxiety about potty training this one! Though she is neurotypical, my second daughter's approach to life is "my way or the highway." Blessedly, this round of potty training also went extremely well, as she was showing all the signs of readiness, plus we were at the beginning of a pandemic with nowhere else to go.

My third and last daughter was born with Down syndrome and a spicy personality like her sisters, and she turned everything that I thought I knew about potty training right on its head. As I approached what I thought was the "right" age to potty train, and the age at which her community preschool said was necessary for advancement into the next class, I realized that Abby was not showing a single sign of readiness. Additionally, her muscles worked differently than her sisters had, with global hypotonia and overall pelvic floor weakness. Her communication style was different than her sisters' had been, with better understanding than verbal expression, and some continued need for alternative communication (signs, switches, and pictures). I took a week off work, prepared like I had with her older sisters by unboxing our floor potties, readying our bathroom book baskets/bubble wands/stickers, and letting everyone in our lives know that we'd be emerging from our house in a week or so! Within a day, I was pulling my hair out, questioning all my experience as a therapist and a mom, and realizing that potty training for my third daughter was going to be nothing like my first two.

As an expert in activities of daily living, I judged myself immensely for not being able to solve the puzzle of potty training Abby using the techniques that had previously worked for me and that I had recommended to so many other parents of children with disabilities through the years. As an "expert" in Abby, I also judged myself heartily that I could not instantly find the key to unlock the door that would lead to success for both of us. I did not know what flexibility would exist at her morning community preschool, nor did I know what might be covered by the IEP at her public school special education program. During that week at home with Abby, I did quickly realize that we were not going to be successful at potty training with reckless abandon, and I began to look for external support. This support came by way of buying multiple books and videos, and subscribing to online support systems. Armed with numerous (costly) resources, I devoured all of the material that I could get my hands on and developed a plan of attack.

As an occupational therapist, one of the things I pride myself on is that, while I may not have all the answers for a family (or myself!), I am an excellent gatherer and synthesizer of resources. At the time that I was desperate for resources, this book you are reading did not yet exist. I spent a lot of time gathering general resources about potty training, general resources about disability, and smashing them together to make space for my daughter in a market that was not developed with her in mind. What I love about *The Adaptive Toolkit for Potty Training Children with Disabilities* is that it was created for families just like mine, with all of the support, understanding, and real-life suggestions and solutions that consider children with many types of disabilities. The combination of Allison Jandu's experience and research with the real-life stories and experiences of the Extra Lucky community creates a resource that does not "other" our children and our families, but acknowledges the different paths that each of us may be on.

While I am happy to say that Abby and I ultimately found a potty training solution that worked for us, I am excited to recommend this book to the families that I work with and encounter in both my professional and personal life. I look forward to seeing many families feel supported in all aspects of potty training their child with complex needs and abilities, with real-life techniques and adaptations as well as the encouragement and enthusiasm of the whole disability community behind them!

Sincerely,

Lora Jackle, OTR/L
Pediatric Occupational Therapist
Marz, Riley, and Abby's Mom

Introduction:
Welcome, We're Glad You're Here!

adaptive[1] *(adjective)*

Providing, contributing to, or marked by adaptation
Example: "The adaptive equipment helped the child achieve independence."

Designed to adjust or respond to different conditions or environments
Example: "The program took an adaptive approach to meet the needs of all learners."

In the disability community, adaptive tools exist everywhere. They are what help our kids fit into a world where they don't always naturally fit. This can look like a wheelchair, an augmentative and alternative communication (AAC) device or, something many of us use, glasses. The end goal is the same—moving about, communicating, seeing clearly—but the adaptation helps us get there. Potty training is no different. In the disability community, potty training principals often have to be modified to get us to where we want to be, which is the independence that toileting can give our children. Our toolkit may just need to be a little bigger.

We know firsthand that potty training can be a very daunting thing to think about pursuing. Will my child's disability affect how they potty train? When should I start? How do I even begin to go about this process? Well, unfortunately, there simply is no miracle potty training cure and no one-size-fits-all way to get the job done. Every child is different, every disability is different, and therefore, every potty training journey is going to be different, too. A large part of why Potty Training Consultant's custom consultations have such a high success rate is because each plan is written specifically for each family based on the child's personality, varying experience with the potty, the family's values and lifestyle, important considerations about specific needs surrounding their disabilities, and many other factors. This book is going to give you all those core tools and practices that you need in order to work toward your goals. Not only that, but we wanted to break it down into digestible sections to make it feel more manageable so it fits easily into your existing lifestyle—you shouldn't have to change your entire way of living just to accommodate potty training! If the process seems easier and more manageable, we know you'll be more likely to commit and see it through. That commitment is such an important factor to help your child through this transition, and this will be reinforced throughout the book. Ultimately, you will be the one making the decisions on how to shape your potty training journey. Allison is the expert on potty training, but you are the expert on your child. As you continue reading, think of ways you can customize your own experience to match your family's unique needs.

About Allison

Welcome to The Adaptive Toolkit for Potty Training Children with Disabilities! My name is Allison Jandu and you probably know me as the owner and founder of Potty Training Consultant, where we have very proudly helped thousands of families reach their potty training goals, saving more than 10 million diapers worldwide!

In addition to being a business owner, my number one job is mom. I have two kids myself, Evan and Layla. When I potty trained them many years ago, it made me realize the lack of reliable resources available to parents who were having a hard time potty training; I decided to become that resource that people could trust. I earned my bachelor of science degree in forensic studies from the University of Baltimore back in 2006, so I have a very strong science background and my mind works in the way of a scientist: I want to know the research and the "why" behind things. I have spent over 5,000 hours researching all things potty training, early childhood development, human behavior and psychology—all of the factors that go into shaping a healthy potty training experience, and I'm continuing that education all the time. I've been honored to contribute extensively to the education of childcare professionals and parents by writing internationally accredited training programs and developing a series of acclaimed online courses. My insights have been featured on major media platforms such as Good Morning America, New York Magazine, and BuzzFeed. In combination with my hands-on experience of working with so many families, each with their own unique circumstances, and a big percentage of them having a child with a disability, I have created a platform where parents can come together in a judgment-free zone, ask those hard questions, and get evidence-based solutions to tackle this challenging, yet amazing milestone.

It's truly an honor to be able to connect and partner with Extra Lucky Moms (ELM) to finally bring you the much needed and much deserved guidance for potty training that you've been missing. Life as an extra lucky parent is already filled with so much uncertainty—keeping track of doctor's visits, therapy progress, medical expenses, insurance battles—not to mention all the emotional ups and downs that come along with this journey. Stressing over potty training shouldn't have to be another thing on your never-ending to-do list or mental load. I've wanted to put together this guide for a very long time, especially after I became an extra lucky mom myself in 2021. My daughter, Layla, was diagnosed with Type 1 Diabetes when she was five years old. This means she now has a lifelong disability because her body can't make its own insulin, and as of right now, there is no cure. Every day, every time she eats, sleeps, or exercises, we have to make a diabetes management decision. Every time we leave the house, we have to carry along a bag of life-saving medical supplies. While her disability might not necessarily be visible, it's something that greatly affects our lives, just like nearly one in ten children worldwide living with a disability.[2]

If there is only one thing you take away from this program, I want it to be that you are not alone. You now have the love, support, and solidarity of Extra Lucky Moms and Potty Training Consultant, and we believe in you!!

About Taryn and Jess

Welcome! We are Taryn Lagonigro and Jess Quarello, co-founders of ELM (originally known as Extra Lucky Moms) and passionate disability advocates. We are mamas to six girls between us! Each of our youngest daughters was born with Down syndrome in 2020, which is what led us to start a movement shifting perspectives in the disability community and the world. The ELM community, now the largest of its kind, represents countless common and rare disabilities, with over 65 million impressions on social media, and still growing! We are established speakers in the disability community, having been frequent guests on podcasts, interviews, and for several corporate diversity and inclusion speaking engagements, including at many large financial institutions. Our work has been featured on The Today Show, multiple CBS affiliates, and many print articles. In 2024, we launched The Extra Lucky Podcast to bring additional resources to the large ELM community, and we were awarded the National Down Syndrome Congress Social Media Award for positively impacting the lives of individuals with Down syndrome through social media.

Taryn is also the founder of Four Clovers Publishing, who published this book. The mission of Four Clovers is to publish inclusive, meaningful, and empowering content that supports, educates, and uplifts communities, particularly those in marginalized populations like the disability community.

Collectively, our personal and professional experience is vast, and we share a mission of supporting caregivers in the disability community and shouting the worth of ALL people.

The creation of this book is more than just a guide; it's a heartfelt message from us— ELM, Jess, and Taryn—to every caregiver and parent who has felt overwhelmed or alone in their journey. We understand the complexities and delicate nuances of raising a child with disabilities. That's why we've poured our experiences and insights into these pages, hoping to simplify and support one of the more challenging milestones: potty training. This book is a culmination of research, personal trials, and parent experiences, crafted to be an ally in your corner. We believe in a world where disability is not a barrier to living a fulfilling life, and we hope this book serves as a testament to that belief and a helpful companion on your caregiving path.

Our drive to create this manual stems from a clear need for specialized resources that address the realities of potty training children with disabilities. As we are developing this book, neither of our children are 100% potty trained and we are able to still see little wins and growth as we continue to work toward potty training independence for our girls. We want to ensure all caregivers recognize their wins, even during the challenging task of potty training.

We've personally experienced the frustration and the lack of tailored guidance available to parents and caregivers. It's our mission to fill this gap with a comprehensive, understanding approach that recognizes the unique challenges faced by these extraordinary and capable individuals. We aim to equip caregivers with knowledge and strategies that are informed by real-life experiences and professional expertise, thanks to Allison and her team. Our vision is for a world where disability doesn't hinder access to education or resources, especially for something as fundamental as potty training. By providing this guide, we're contributing to a larger movement of inclusivity and support within the caregiving community.

Potty training is more than just a milestone—it's a gateway to independence and confidence. This book offers more than instructions—it's a tool to empower children and caregivers to master a vital life skill at their own pace and in their own way. We focus on adaptive strategies that are sensitive to individual needs, encouraging progress without pressure. Our approach is centered on celebrating small victories and fostering a sense of achievement, which is essential for building self-esteem in all kids. By enabling individuals to overcome challenges associated with potty training, we're contributing to their overall growth and helping them unlock their full potential in all areas of life. The goal may not be 100% independence, but there will always be growth to celebrate and we want to make sure all caregivers see that in their commitment to helping their children grow and learn.

Thank you for allowing us to be a part of this milestone. You are here, ready to learn insights to help your Extra Lucky person succeed. We are here with you, holding space for you and celebrating the big, small, and everything in between.

And don't forget, you've got this!

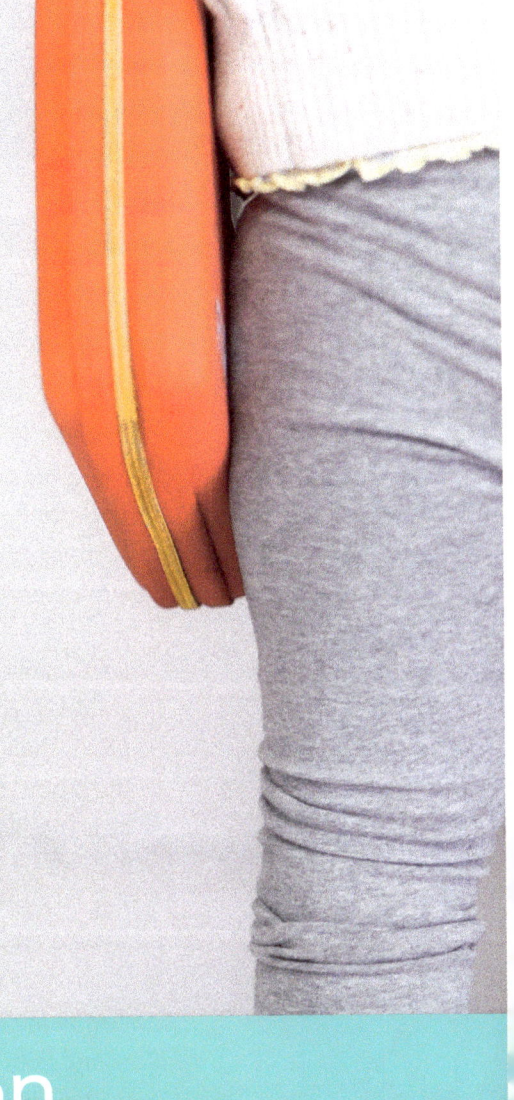

GETTING READY TO GO

Preparation

Chapter 1: Mental Prep

For Parents

Potty training is generally a daunting milestone for any parent to think about taking on, but for parents of a child with a disability, it can feel like a massive undertaking. Your journey will often require more time and patience, not to mention coming up with specialized approaches to meet your child at their unique level of ability, which can further increase your stress and anxiety about starting the process.

It's something we hear all the time: every child is unique. And when a child has a disability, this is even more important to take into consideration. Their physical, cognitive, or sensory differences can render standard potty training methods ineffective and frustrating. For example, if your child's disability comes along with sensory processing issues, they might find the sensation of just sitting on a toilet overwhelming. This leaves you thinking, "How am I supposed to get them potty trained when they won't even sit on the toilet?!"

Communication delays and challenges can add another layer of complexity. Children with disabilities might struggle to express when they need to go or understand instructions enough to manage the steps of using the potty. Adapting your approach to match your child's needs by using visual aids (which we will touch on more in Chapter 8), sign language, or assistive technology like AAC devices can bridge this gap. Speech therapists can provide valuable tools and techniques to enhance communication skills, making the process smoother and less frustrating for both you and your child.

Children with developmental delays or disabilities may not be ready for potty training at the same age as their peers, and in some cases, it could even be years later. This can feel disheartening when you may feel pressure from unrealistic societal expectations and comparisons. It's so important to give yourself grace and remember that every child develops at their own pace! Surround yourself with supportive people who understand your journey, such as other parents of children with disabilities or support groups like ELM, to remind you that you are not alone.

Health-related issues can significantly complicate potty training. Some children with disabilities may have medical conditions that affect bladder or bowel control, making the process more complex and leave you wondering whether potty training is even in the cards for your child. Regular checkups with your child's healthcare team can help manage these issues and make you feel more comfortable about their physical readiness.

Finally, I fully acknowledge that the emotional toll of potty training can be significant. The process can be exhausting, especially when progress seems slow or setbacks occur. It's easy to feel discouraged, but keep reminding yourself that potty training is a process, not a one-time event. It's okay to focus on one step of the process at a time, to take breaks when needed, and to lean on your child's care team for support and guidance. Doctors, therapists, teachers, and even family members can offer different perspectives and expertise to help you. Sometimes having emotional support is most important, so try to find someone who can occasionally remind you that it's okay to ask for help and take time for yourself. Remember, you are doing an incredible job, and every small step forward is a victory worth celebrating!

For Children

Before embarking on this journey with your child, it can be helpful to understand why and how potty training can be just as overwhelming from their perspective, if not more so, as it is from your own. Using the potty instead of diapers is a major transition for every child, so it's important to look at things from their point of view to help you approach the process with a supportive and patient mindset.

First, consider if your child has a physical disability or mobility challenges. Using the potty is a complex physical act involving a variety of gross and fine motor skills. Your child needs to get to the bathroom, undress, get up onto the toilet, coordinate their pelvic floor muscles to release their bladder and/or bowels, wipe (or be wiped), get down from the toilet, dress again, flush, wash hands—even I'm tired from writing all the steps! Add mobility challenges to the mix and you might find that your child has a hard time making it to the bathroom in time or maneuvering themselves up onto the toilet on their own. This can be frustrating and discouraging for them, making the whole process feel stressful instead of empowering.

I will be talking about this a lot throughout the book, but for children with sensory processing disorders, the sensations associated with using the toilet—such as the feeling of toilet paper or the sound of flushing—can be overwhelming or even scary. Remember, this whole process is a brand new experience, so they don't necessarily know what to expect. These kids may be more likely to resist using the bathroom if it feels too uncomfortable or stressful for them.

Communication difficulties can also pose challenges. Children who have trouble expressing their needs or understanding instructions may struggle to convey when they need to use the bathroom. They may also get frustrated by being taken to the potty when they don't actually need to go, which can result in resistance and pushback. Occasionally, kids who struggle to effectively communicate can resort to lashing out with tantrums or even aggressive behaviors like hitting or biting. If this happens, try to keep in mind that your child likely feels that they are all out of resources to get you to understand them. Much like the popular parenting quote, your child isn't giving you a hard time, they are having a hard time.

Lastly, just like with parents and caregivers, the emotional impact of potty training should not be taken lightly! Children with disabilities already face more challenges than most people in their daily lives, and adding the pressure of potty training can feel like yet another project. That's why it's so important to approach potty training gradually, with empathy and realistic goals, while reassuring your child that it's okay to make mistakes and that they are loved and supported no matter what.

Pep Talk

Before we really get started, I want to give you a little bit of a pep talk. I fully understand and acknowledge that most parents look forward to the end result of potty training—not having to change diapers anymore—but they do not look forward to the actual process of potty training, itself. When your child has a disability, you might even think that you'll be changing diapers for way longer or that potty training isn't even possible for your child. Well, I'm here to let you know that just because your child has a disability, does not always mean that you have to majorly postpone potty training! A disability doesn't necessarily equal a disadvantage, and one thing you can look forward to in this book is necessary accommodations that match your child's specific needs. Of course, there are some key physical and developmental factors that would ideally be established before you get started, which we'll talk about more in a bit.

For the most part, initiating potty training is going to be all about your readiness to tackle this new milestone. Give your child and yourself some grace. Potty training doesn't have to be something that's dreadful and anxiety-inducing, that's all packed into one weekend. Potty training can actually be a really awesome opportunity to bond with your child, and it can be done gradually over time at a pace that is comfortable for you both.

When I'm working with a family one-on-one, I always take some time to make sure they have the right mindset as they are embarking (or for some, re-embarking) on the journey to diaper freedom. You'll want to be sure to set realistic expectations going into this. First, it's important that you not compare your experience to anyone else's experience.

Not a family with a child who doesn't have a disability, not a family with a child who has the same disability—your child is going to have their own potty training experience, and that is normal! The way it goes for you, whether it's super hard or super easy, happens over a weekend, takes years, or your child is never 100% independent, is not a reflection on you or your parenting (or your child!). Second, it's important to understand what potty training truly is. Repeat after me: *Potty training is a process, not an event.* It is a combination of multi-faceted learned skills and behaviors. There is a lot that goes into using the potty independently! The learning process is likely going to have bad days mixed in with good days, and that should be expected. Try to always find those glimmers of progress and success and focus on those. Potty training progress is not measured by the number of accidents, but by your child's understanding of this new skill. Mistakes will be made along the way, and, believe it or not, that is when the most learning is taking place. Also, success looks different for everyone—it's not always about pee and poop getting in the potty. For some kids, they need to start off with just being in the bathroom environment, getting comfortable sitting on the potty, or releasing without a diaper on. Keeping these things in mind as you are down in the trenches should help you feel more confident and committed.

Consistency

All children thrive with well-established routines and schedules, and that can be especially true for children with disabilities due to some of the unique challenges they might face on a daily basis. Routines bring feelings of safety and security, which is why it's important to establish consistency surrounding potty training, too! Being consistent with your routines, language, and expectations about potty use can make it easier for your child to grasp the concept, understand the process, and ultimately successfully use the potty. Consistency also helps to reinforce positive behaviors and minimize confusion for your child, which can be even more important for kids who struggle with communication or understanding complex sets of instructions. When you are able to maintain a consistent approach to potty training, you and your child's care team can create a positive, supportive, and reliable environment that will lead to potty confidence and independence.

Mindset for the Caregiver

A note from Taryn: As a yoga and meditation instructor long before being part of the disability community, I understand how important mindset is. We intentionally wanted to include elements of that throughout this book. Potty training *any* child can often be a stressful journey, and our children's disabilities can add some complexities to that process. There can be parts of it that are hard to accept, and that doesn't make you a bad parent, that makes you human. Whether your child needs adaptive clothing or tools, is among typical peers who have been toilet trained for a while, or if you're tired of bringing a diaper bag everywhere you go, we see you. Celebrate your little wins and also give yourself a moment from time to time to acknowledge the *hard,* especially all the hard work you're doing. In the back of this book are mantras and meditations for the potty training caregiver. I hope you remember to come back to them when you need a boost or a moment to yourself.

Remember to practice ways to keep a positive mindset regularly, however that looks for you, to cultivate inner peace, strength, and resilience throughout your potty training journey.

The Value of a Support System

A note from Jess and Taryn, ELM: There is power in community through our journey of parenting our children with disabilities. While there are many ups and downs, potty training being only one of them, the one thing that has always made a difference is the support of our community.

You see, when you're part of a community, you're never alone. There are people who understand exactly what you're going through, who validate your experiences, and who offer invaluable insights and resources. Nobody should ever feel isolated or overwhelmed as a caregiver or parent. Drawing from our own experiences, we've found immense strength and camaraderie among individuals who are facing similar challenges. It's through shared experiences that we've learned the most and received the most genuine support.

So, if you're in a similar situation, we encourage you to find community, even if it is just one person you can lean on. ELM is a warm and welcoming space filled with real stories, practical resources, and a sense of belonging. Here, you can learn from others, share your own insights, and gather the courage and knowledge you need to tackle the potty training journey with patience and resilience.

Leaning in, especially to someone that truly understands your experiences, can be life-changing. This is where you can find strength, hope, and a shared wisdom that lights up your path through the complexities of disability parenting. ELM is one such example, and we are here to embrace you, educate you, and empower you every step of the way.

Taryn and Rhea:
Reluctancy and Pride

When we started conversations with Allison, The Potty Training Consultant, and the rest of the team to put this book together, I didn't realize how much the process would help me in real time. Spending weekly or bi-weekly sessions talking about potty training really motivated me to get out of my own way about taking the journey with my daughter, Rhea, who was born with Down syndrome in 2020.

Rhea is the youngest of four girls, and there are many ways that being a "veteran mom" has prepared me well for this life raising a child with a disability. There are also many ways that she has thrown the book out as far as things I thought I knew, potty training being one of them. My three older children all potty trained differently, yet still followed many of the traditional methods. My oldest daughter was the tried and true version of "when she's ready, she will do it" and loved rewards. My bigger middle basically potty trained herself when she turned 2; motivated by her older sister, she wanted to be a big girl and she let me know that. My third took a while, but ultimately responded best to a timer method. Ironically, I thought she would be the easiest since we did it during COVID-19 with nothing else to do but stay home.

If Rhea hadn't been born with a disability, potty training the youngest of four children would have likely still been a challenge. Once the pandemic was mostly behind us, our life returned to an even busier version of the one before it. Four kids' worth of sports, activities, and my own schedule meant finding large chunks of time (or the elusive "free weekend") to potty train would be difficult.

But when Rhea approached the traditional potty training age, I got in my head about way more than just our busy life. I knew from the lived experience of parents in the disability community around me that this piece of the journey could be tough, and I let that stop me from wanting to try. Her teachers and therapists would comment on her readiness, but I would make halfhearted efforts and get immediately overwhelmed.

I wasn't simply being negative about the process—I happen to know my kid very well. There are many ways that Rhea's development is typical of her age, but one big gap I notice as I raise her as an older toddler is in generalization: she hasn't always shown me she's connecting the dots between one situation and another. We have struggled with how to appropriately discipline her, because positive or negative reinforcement doesn't always carry over to the next time she goes to do the same thing.

You can see why, then, when it comes to something like potty training, I was at a loss. How do I potty train a kid when I am unsure whether rewards or consequences will resonate with her?

I didn't start to find the answer until I sent Rhea to summer camp at her former daycare in the summer of 2024. Rhea was in a class with neurotypical peers, most of whom completed potty training. The classroom followed a routine in which everyone went to the bathroom on a predictable schedule. Rhea came home after the first week having had zero accidents. I realized that what had been missing in my tries before was consistency, repetition, and predictability...something easier said than done in a family of six.

That weekend, I had to give myself a bit of a mindset shift. (My own journey is a big reason why we talk a lot about mindset in this book!). The effort that consistency would take would be worth it for what potty training success would give us. I had to stop looking at the mountain to climb and start looking at what was on the other side of it. We committed to going all in and haven't looked back. While I knew we would use disposable training pants for a long time at night, I tried to not let the hard days land us back there in the daytime. I bought Rhea super-thick training underwear that minimized mess with accidents, and we did our best to ensure we were taking her to the potty on a regular basis, including when we were out or having any other disruption to our schedule.

As I write this, we are about 80% there, which is quite honestly 80% further than I thought we would be six months ago. This disability journey has taught me to lean hard on dialectical thinking (what we more casually call "the and concept"). The 20% can still feel hard and we can celebrate the wins. We may be prompting her for a while and it has gotten easier. Success for Rhea may never be 100% and she will still have independence. Our current goals involve her letting those around her know when she needs to go, so we can start to build that habit and have greater success in environments where the routine of parents or teachers asking her isn't there.

We still have days where it feels like we have a ways to go and I'm really proud of how far we have come. The effort is worth it for the result. And Rhea is always worth the effort.

Chapter 2:
Getting Everyone On Board

Knowing that children with disabilities often require a multifaceted approach to address their unique needs, you can bring the entire care team together to customize different therapies, strategies, and interventions to provide your child with the best care possible. Each person on the team will likely have their own contribution based on not just your child's challenges, but also their capabilities. So by keeping open communication and coordination across the board, you'll be better able to really promote your child's overall development and well-being. All of this applies when it's time to start thinking about potty training, too.

Keeping everyone in the loop starting from well before you begin potty training your child is so important, so you can really provide that consistent, reliable experience that we've already talked about in Chapter 1. Not only that, but your child's doctors, therapists, and teachers will have valuable input to help you tailor the potty training experience for your child's unique needs based on their specific areas of expertise. For example, healthcare providers may help identify any important medical-related considerations that could impact your child's potty use, such as physical limitations (hypotonia, lack of urge sensitivity, or constipation, for example) or even sensory sensitivities. Your child's therapists might have unique insight into your child's preferences and behaviors, or tips regarding communication during potty training.

Another layer of complication may be introduced if you and your child's other parent happen to be divorced and live in separate homes. Studies suggest that parents of children with disabilities have a slightly higher divorce rate than that of the general population, so this is very common, and you certainly aren't alone. Keep in mind that shifting between two environments with different routines and expectations can make it harder for your child to adjust, especially if they're already navigating the associated challenges of their disability. Your child may feel confused or anxious about the changes, which can affect their progress. That's why consistency across both households is so important—it helps create a sense of stability for your child, making the potty training process less stressful and more predictable. Consider creating a unified potty training plan that both parents can easily follow. Also, a shared calendar or regular check-ins can help ensure everyone stays on the same page, creating a more supportive experience for your child.

Occasionally, schools have certain rules or requirements when it comes to potty training. You want to find out what these things are before starting your process at home so you can take them into account as you come up with your plan. Most schools have professionals on staff that are excited and incredibly well-equipped to help your child succeed with using the potty while in their care, but still, ask questions, like:

- *Is potty training supported in my child's classroom? Will an aide be available to help?* Sometimes your child has to be in a certain age-level classroom to receive potty access. If you are thinking of starting on the younger side but they aren't in a classroom that works on potty training, it's probably best to wait until they are before pulling the plug on diapers at home, to maintain consistency and avoid confusion. You may need to have potty training outlined in their IEP or 504 plan so your child is guaranteed to receive the individualized support needed to be successful while they are at school. We will have more information on requesting this type of support in Chapter 17.

- **How does using the potty work when my child is in class?** Some schools have set times when every child lines up to use the potty, some schools have it on an as-needed basis only, and some schools require that a child be fully self-sufficient with their potty use from self-initiation all the way through wiping and redressing.

- **What is the accident policy?** Most schools are fairly accommodating as far as changing a child's clothes when they have an accident. However, some may require that a child wear disposable training underwear if they have a certain number of accidents. They might be sent to the health room to be changed, they might request that you come in to change your child or send them home for the day, or they might require that your child remain in disposable training underwear altogether while at school until they can prove to be accident-free for a specified number of days.

- **Can you help me document potty habits and observations?** Having as much information available as possible across all environments can help you identify patterns or learn where adjustments might be needed in order to continue making progress. It's always an added bonus if your child's caregiver is willing to document times that the potty was attempted, times it was used successfully, when accidents occurred, notable progress made, and more.

As you're thinking about getting started with potty training, arrange some meetings or phone calls with everyone on the care team, including other family members. Maintain that communication throughout the process as well so everyone can contribute information about your child's wins and areas of improvement to keep progress advancing. Creating a simple progress chart to help you document things you notice about your child's potty habits and preferences that can be easily distributed throughout the care team can keep everyone on the same page. Here is what your progress chart might look like:

Potty Progress Chart

You can scan the QR code to download and copy this chart to keep track of your child's potty progress, behaviors, and preferences. You can then pass along this information to their caregivers to keep things as consistent as possible.

How frequently does your child pee?	
How much liquid does your child drink before peeing?	
How often does your child poop?	
What time of day does your child normally poop?	
How does your child show that they need to use the potty?	
What are your child's potty preferences (privacy vs company, books vs songs, etc)?	
Are there any sensory considerations?	
What rewards are you using?	
How do you respond to accidents?	

www.pottytrainingchildrenwithdisabilities.com

A collaborative approach empowers caregivers when they have a solid understanding of your potty training plan and goals, which promotes a successful and rewarding experience for everyone involved!

Above all, remember that you are your child's greatest advocate. It's important to ensure that each member of their care team is not only a good fit but also provides the proper support, care, and resources your child needs. Don't hesitate to ask questions, seek out second opinions, or adjust the team if necessary; your child's success and comfort always come first. With a strong, supportive team in place, your child will be well on their way to potty training progress.

The Care Team: Supportive Roles

In addition to having support for yourself, you will most likely have a dedicated care team ready to support your child's progress. From occupational therapists and speech-language pathologists to behavioral specialists and dietitians, each professional brings unique expertise that can address the associated traits or challenges your child may face. This collaborative approach ensures you and your child receive the guidance and reassurance you both deserve. We all know it takes a village to raise a child, and that is especially true if your child happens to have a disability. Try to keep in mind that potty training doesn't have to fall entirely on your shoulders alone.

Let's discuss some of the most common people that may have a supportive role in your child's potty training journey.

> When thinking about your child's care team, it is important to know who your experts are. Because they are all experts in their respective fields, you can lean on each of them differently to support where you are in the potty training process. Most experts designate specialization in pediatric versus adult care, so be sure you're accessing someone who has experience working with children.

Occupational Therapy

Occupational therapists (OTs) help children develop the skills they need for everyday tasks, like getting dressed, eating, playing, or using the potty. They are your experts in sensory processing and adaptive equipment, focusing on improving fine motor skills, coordination, and overall sensory integration to make daily activities easier and more enjoyable for your child. Whether it's helping them strengthen their grip to hold a pencil or teaching them how to manage sensory sensitivities, OTs create fun, hands-on strategies that help kids become more independent and confident in their abilities.

Physical Therapy

Physical therapists (PTs) help children improve their movement, strength, and coordination. They are your experts in questions about motor control, transfers, mobility, and the pelvic floor. When it comes to potty training, they can play a big role in helping your child develop the necessary physical skills, like balance, core strength, and the ability to sit or stand safely while using the potty. PTs use fun exercises and activities designed just for kids, helping them build up the muscles and skills they need to move more easily.

Speech-Language Pathology

Speech-language pathologists (SLPs) are specialists who help children with communication challenges. They are your experts in communication, both verbal and alternative, and will work with your child on developing these skills. An SLP can also assist with feeding and swallowing issues, which can be common in children with disabilities. By using fun, personalized strategies, they will help your child build confidence and develop the skills they need to communicate in their own ways.

Behaviorists, Psychologists, and Counselors

A behaviorist is a professional who focuses on behavior and how it can be shaped or changed to improve daily life. They are your experts in studying and identifying actions and how they relate to environmental stimuli. They will look at how your child responds to different situations and work with both them and you to create strategies that encourage positive behaviors and reduce challenging ones. While a behaviorist might seem similar to a psychologist or counselor, the key difference is that behaviorists usually focus more on specific actions and behaviors, whereas psychologists or counselors often dive deeper into emotions and overall mental health. Many kids can benefit from support in navigating their feelings and emotions in addition to addressing observable behaviors. Each of these professionals can be a great support for children with disabilities, but their approaches may differ depending on your child's needs.

Nutritionists and Dietitians

A nutritionist or dietitian is a professional who helps individuals make sure they're getting the right nutrition to support their growth and overall health. They are your experts in digestive health when it comes to potty training. They can create personalized meal plans to address any specific dietary needs or challenges, like food allergies or sensitivities that could be common in children with disabilities. During potty training, their services can be especially helpful if your child is struggling with constipation or other digestive issues.

Meg and Cammie: Defying Expectations

Cammie is an amazing little girl who is four years old and has Down syndrome. After months of researching toilet training, I was left feeling very overwhelmed and, quite frankly, pretty defeated at the thought of starting this process. However, I have some good news! Despite some obstacles and special considerations, Cammie was potty trained in two months at the age of three!

It is sometimes difficult to know when to start the toilet training journey with your child with Down syndrome. Cammie actually showed interest in using the potty, but this isn't always the case. I made it my job as her mom to become the "Potty Tour Director," and I was going to make this experience as fun and carefree as possible. I'm going to be very honest here, though: there are very few shortcuts during this potty journey. It takes a lot of time, commitment, and perseverance, which means the parent (along with teachers and caregivers) must be emotionally and physically ready to ensure success.

In the beginning of our potty journey, we would play pretend. She would always sit her dolls or her favorite Bluey toy on the toilet, and I would make the sound of them going to the potty. We would then have a potty celebration dance afterward, which she absolutely loved! We also started to read a lot of books about going to the potty, and she was very interested in coming with me to the bathroom.

I feel extremely blessed because her team's philosophy at school is that all kids deserve to be exposed to toileting and given the chance to succeed, so they start all kids sitting on the toilet twice a day. I learned so much from them during this potty training experience last year. They believe that giving the children an expectation and talking through what the toilet means is so important. Many students in her class have sensory regulation concerns, which means they don't always know what different sensations mean or even how to detect that they have to go to the bathroom. So, exposing them by sitting on the toilet puts their bodies in a natural position to use the bathroom. Over time, they start to connect the feeling of sitting with having to eliminate. From the very beginning, Cammie was very interested in the toilet. It became a routine we did every day at home and at school. We talked about whether her diaper was wet or dry and discussed pushing the pee and poop out. Once she peed for the first time, she was excited to go to the bathroom and wanted to be in there often, which was a clue she was ready. It was very important for Cammie to communicate with me when she had to go. For Cammie, it was the potty sign combined with her saying, "eee" for "pee." I want to reiterate how important this language aspect is. Everyone on this potty journey with your child must speak the same language. I worked as a team with her teachers, and we all made sure to use the same ASL sign for potty and the same words when we took her to the bathroom. Consistency was absolutely essential for Cammie's success!

From there, we used a daily progress sheet at home and at school. We used this to record her progress and note the times of day she was frequenting the restroom. Over the next month, the data was recorded, and it was wonderful to see how the successes for the month increased. It was working, and she was staying dry more and more each day.

The bump we ran into was her emptying her bladder. This isn't uncommon. Since Cammie has Down syndrome and low muscle tone, it makes sense that she would also have low muscle tone in her pelvic floor. Cammie would get impatient and would only pee a little, then sign that she had to go to the bathroom 15 minutes later. Because of her low tone, she didn't know how to empty her bladder completely. Either way, it was something she had to learn how to do. I would set a timer and let her read a new book on the toilet while she waited. Another important factor for Cammie was waiting to celebrate until after she peed. If you celebrated too soon at the beginning of her going pee, she would get too excited and stop her flow. Eventually, we could celebrate after she completely emptied her bladder and didn't need the timer. Proper position was also imperative for Cammie to empty her bladder. We used a child-sized toilet seat with a footstool so she felt secure with her feet firmly supported. Cammie needed to feel safe and balanced so she could relax and concentrate on going to the bathroom.

With time, Cammie's body and brain made the connection through consistency and repeated practice. Now, Cammie loves being independent and initiates the toileting routine, which means she recognizes the need to go to the bathroom and goes! I still have to help Cammie in some ways, but the ultimate goal is independent toileting without help from others. We are slowly getting there. So, I guess the moral of the story is patience, patience, more patience, and steady persistence. Keep a sense of humor about it, keep it stress-free, and if all else fails, you can start again tomorrow! Once the lightbulb goes off and your child knows what is expected, they can be successful—and the sky's the limit! They just need that confidence, self-esteem, and belief in themselves to help them soar and succeed in their potty journey. You've got this!

Chapter 3: When to Start

Signs of Readiness

Before we dive into the actual potty training itself, let's first take some time to review how to determine the ideal time to start this process, which will be different for each family based on a number of unique factors. There are many things that can influence when the best time is to start potty training for your family specifically, including:

- Your child's developmental readiness
- Any other changes or transitions that may be happening around the same time
- Support from other caregivers
- Your readiness
- Signs of Readiness
- Age Is Just a Number

First, and probably most importantly, I want to focus on a few critical signs of readiness that your child may display so you can be confident that they are physically, cognitively, and emotionally ready for this new phase. Starting when your child is displaying some or all of these signs can make the entire process go much more smoothly. There are some signs that are more obvious than others, and some that you may not have even thought to connect with potty training before, so let's discuss those now.

The first thing most people tend to think of when deciding if a child is ready for potty training is their age. When a child has a disability, this tends to shift the typical age of readiness to be later than for neurotypical children. For example, a 2002 study[3] showed that children with autism tend to complete potty training at age 36 months, with 5% still having accidents at age 12 years. Another study from 2022[4] showed that children with Down syndrome start at age 3.4 years and finish by 5.88 years, whereas the average ideal age to start potty training for a neurotypical child is between ages 18 to 24 months, according to the American Academy of Pediatrics.[5]

Important to note is there are several variables that could push your child's ideal age window one way or another. Therefore, instead of putting so much focus on age alone, which can often put even more pressure on caregivers to accomplish potty training within a preconceived window, I highly encourage families to think about developmental readiness. According to scholar Mia E. Lang, "...potty training is a very complex skill integrating physiological and behavioral processes."[6] So, depending on a child's development, potty training is going to happen at all different ages. Don't listen to those other sources that may make you feel like you've somehow failed if you "waited too long" or "missed the opportunity." The truth is, when a child has a disability, they may never be fully independent with toileting, and that has nothing to do with the age at which your child began potty training.

Developmental Signs of Readiness

We've decided to not focus on your child's age, so how can you determine when might be a good time to start potty training? When your child has a disability, it's important to take a gradual approach to potty training, starting off with a strong foundation of basic needs and prerequisites. By focusing first on things like poop regulation and posture, then moving on to body awareness and routine, you can set your child up for long-term success before moving on to the more advanced skills like self-initiation, independent potty use, and wiping. Let's talk about some of the developmental signs you might begin to notice from your child that could indicate a readiness to start potty training.

Advancing gross motor skills. Meeting milestones, like sitting, standing, and walking is helpful before starting to use the potty without assistance, and that is mainly for safety reasons. Some children with physical disabilities won't be at this point now or ever, and even one day can look different from the next, and that is okay, too. This just means that they may require more assistance as they're learning. If your child does struggle with physical or mobility challenges, it is important to get clearance from their doctors and physical therapists first to be sure that using the potty is within your child's current capabilities.

Physiological health. We also want to ensure that kids are ready for potty training from an internal standpoint. It isn't fair to expect them to use the potty if their bladder, bowels, core, and pelvic floor haven't matured enough to do so. This can be the main reason for a delay in potty training readiness among children with disabilities. Many diagnoses can be accompanied by symptoms such as hypertonia or hypotonia, which can affect a child's ability to hold or void their bladder and bowels effectively. The best way to determine this is to make note of how many wet diapers they have throughout the day and how often. Ideally, they should be able to keep their diaper dry for approximately an hour or more during the day. You'll likely also notice some changes to their poop habits. They probably won't be pooping overnight anymore (pooping in their nighttime diaper first thing in the morning doesn't count!), they have likely consolidated their bowel movements into one or two poops per day, and they may have some predictability when it comes to pooping. Some parents are accurately able to predict what time of day they tend to poop or at least how frequently they go. If you haven't noticed any patterns yet, don't worry. It can be helpful to keep a calendar by your changing station so you can keep some notes.

Expressive and receptive communication. Some level of expressive communication, meaning being able to express a need, is helpful, even if it isn't through spoken words. Nonverbal children might be able to use sign language, gestures, visual supports, or an AAC device. Your child should also have some level of receptive language skills, meaning they can understand what you are telling them, at least in simple form. If they can understand and follow a simple one- or two-step instruction, they can more easily learn and comprehend the steps of using the potty themselves. Generally, kids who are delayed with speech, language, and communication are also delayed with starting potty training. If your child isn't yet able to effectively communicate, it may be best to hold off on starting potty training to avoid added frustration for both you and them.

Social awareness. From a social standpoint, it's always beneficial if a child is showing awareness or curiosity about other people's behavior. Maybe you've noticed that they sometimes try to mimic what you're doing, like walking the dog or washing the dishes, or they are showing a newfound independence by trying to put on their own shoes or feeding themselves. This can all be used to your advantage during the potty learning phase, because right now they are eager to copy and do things they see adults or their peers doing. You might find your child wanting to take a turn sitting on the toilet after you go or sitting on a small potty across from you while you go, which becomes a great learning opportunity.

Potty-Related Signs of Readiness

Let's start talking about some of the "potty specific" signs of readiness you might witness from your child. These are all optional, meaning they aren't required to be present in order to start the process, but if they are, that's a great bonus.

General interest. The most common thing caregivers tend to notice is that the child starts to show some general interest in the bathroom, or in their own bodily functions. They might start following you into the bathroom when you go, show curiosity, play with the toilet paper, flush the toilet, put things into the toilet, and so on. You might also observe them starting to take their diaper off after they've peed or pooped, or even playing with their poop or private parts. Some children are sensory seekers, which could lead to fecal smearing (e.g., playing with their poop, squeezing it between their fingers, smearing it on walls or bedding, or even trying to taste it, which I'll cover more in Chapter 14). It's important to not overreact to these behaviors, as horrifying as they might seem to us when we are in the moment. Your child most likely doesn't understand that they've done anything wrong—and really, they haven't—as they are genuinely just curious and exploring things they were never aware of before. These behaviors, while frustrating, are very normal and are great conversation starters for what poop is or what certain body parts are and their purpose. Giving too much attention or having a great big reaction could unintentionally cause the behavior to happen more often.

Noticing a wet or soiled diaper. Another great indicator of being ready to use the potty is if your child understands and communicates about having peed or pooped in their diaper. They may tell you that they are going while it's happening, or they may ask to have their diaper changed when it's wet or soiled. For children who aren't verbal, this could look like tugging at a full diaper or indicating some form of discomfort, or grabbing a new diaper and bringing it to you when they need changing. Any or all of these actions show an increased level of body awareness and possibly urge recognition, too, which are huge aspects of potty training. If they are able to communicate these things to you, it is also a great time to start teaching them some of the vocabulary surrounding potty training.

Hiding to poop. If your child hides when they're having a bowel movement in their diaper—whether it be behind the couch, in their bedroom closet, or even just covering their face in the corner—or if they become very sensitive to your presence when they are trying to go or have just gone, such as yelling at you to stay away from them, not wanting to be touched until they're done pooping, or resisting diaper changes afterwards, these are great signs that they are ready to start potty training. Why? It shows that they know they need to go, so they recognize that urge in their body, and they know to take a certain action before it happens. If they can move to their favorite hiding spot before letting their poop come out, then in theory, they can move to the potty instead!

Now remember, this isn't a checklist that needs to be marked off before you can begin the process. In fact, you can start introducing the concept of the potty to your child as young as you'd like! You don't have to wait to start talking about potty training right when you want to ditch the diapers. It's much better if you can familiarize your child and provide some positive, stress-free exposure at as young of an age as possible so that it is less of a huge transition later on.

READY TO "GO"?

Developmental Readiness
- ✓ Advancing Gross Motor Skills
- ✓ Physiological Health
- ✓ Expressive & Receptive Communication
- ✓ Social Awareness

Potty Readiness
- ✓ General Interest
- ✓ Noticing a Wet or Soiled Diaper
- ✓ Hiding to Poop

Remember, this list does not have to be completely checked off to start, but rather includes general signs that it's time to introduce the potty!

Caregiver Support

As we discussed in Chapter 2, having caregiver support during potty training is absolutely essential, especially for children with disabilities. Potty training isn't just a solo job for you—it's a team effort, and having the right support can make all the difference. This means making sure your child's caregivers, whether that's a grandparent, teacher, or childcare provider, are on the same page and ready to help create a consistent, supportive learning environment. Before diving in, it's a good idea to check with everyone on your child's care team to ensure they're able and available to offer the right kind of support. This can help everyone stay in sync and ensure your child is getting the guidance and reinforcement they need, no matter where they are. When the whole team is on board, the potty training journey can feel much smoother for everyone!

Timing It Right

Just as important as looking for signs that your child is ready to begin potty training is that you begin at a time that makes sense for your family. Potty training affects the family as a whole and involves a lot of coordination among your child's caregivers. You're going to want to be sure that, if possible, there are no other major changes or transitions happening within your family (e.g., welcoming a new baby, moving to a new home, going on vacation) or with your child themselves (e.g., starting school for the first time, changing therapists, or switching from a crib to a bed). Any type of change or disruption in your child's life has the potential to cause them emotional stress. Emotional stress can lead to regressive behavior, power struggles, or meltdowns when they are faced with too much at one time. Children with disabilities may also struggle to communicate these feelings, which then translates into shifts in behavior. You'll hear me say this a lot, but all children are creatures of habit. Children with disabilities especially thrive on routine and knowing what to expect, as this is what helps them to feel safe, grounded, and in control. If things are already being disrupted, throwing potty training in on top of another life change isn't going to set them up for the best success possible. I always recommend leaving a minimum eight-week buffer period between another life change and potty training. Overall, we just want things to settle down, allowing space to create a new routine for one change before moving on to the next.

Make Sure You Are Ready

I've covered some things you can look for as far as your child's readiness but believe it or not, your readiness as your child's newly appointed potty teacher and coach is just as important! We already talked quite a bit about being in the right mindset as you enter this process and keeping your expectations realistic. You also want to make sure that you feel prepared. Potty training is a big change for your child, yes, but it's a big change for you, too! In fact, it affects the entire family and/or caregiving team as a whole. The initial part of potty training could be messy and inconvenient. It can be stressful and tiring. It can be met with challenges and setbacks. Having a plan in place for how to tackle all of this before you begin will only further ensure that you remain confident and committed so you come out successful on the other side.

Trust Your Instincts

There are occasions when, as the expert on your child, you have to trust your intuition about their capability to tackle potty training. You may be getting pressure from others to begin potty training when you know deep down they just aren't ready. On the flip side, you might know they are ready despite the advice of others. Plenty of children never show clear signs of readiness for potty training, and in those instances, you have to fall back on what your gut is telling you is the right path forward for them. No one knows your child better than you!

Chapter 4:
Preparing for "Go Time"

I can't stress enough how important the preparation portion of the process is to achieving potty success. Potty training isn't necessarily a developmental milestone or something your child will just eventually do on their own. Potty training is a learned skill and a complex one at that! I like to compare potty training to learning how to read. When you're teaching your child how to read, you don't just hand them a book and expect them to figure it out over the course of a weekend. You have to start with the basics, like learning the alphabet, then letter sounds, then blending those sounds, eventually reading short words. Reading the whole book doesn't come until much later after lots of practice and lots of mistakes made along the way. Potty training is the same! You can't just put on underwear and hand your child a potty and expect it to be all figured out within a couple of days. You have to start by establishing a strong foundation to build upon, which will keep the process much less overwhelming for both you and your child.

Intentional Introductions

Most children, especially those with a disability, often thrive on pre-dictability and routine. In addition, changes and transitions can be challenging. So, diving into a huge change like potty training with no preparation or advance notice can lead to resistance, power struggles, stress and frustration, or even anxiety. We want your child to feel prepared *before* entering into this new transition as they are saying goodbye to their old dependable friend, the diaper, and hello to their brand new friend, the potty. Introducing the concept of potty training, providing exposure to the toilet and bathroom, and normalizing our bodily functions from as young of an age as possible all contribute to your child being comfortable, starting with an open mind and minimal fear, resistance, or uncertainty. The goal is to get them on board with the potty in fun, stress-free ways that don't force them to do or change anything themselves right off the bat. It should feel like something that you are doing *with* your child, not *to* your child. Progress can come without pressure!

No matter how old your child is or where they are developmentally, the things we are going to talk about in this part of the guide are all things that you can start doing *right now* to make your eventual potty training journey easier. Potty prep is going to look different for every family, but I would recommend doing at least some, if not all, of the following activities for a minimum of two weeks before saying good-bye to diapers.

Positive Poop Associations

Without even thinking about it, we might use words when we change our child's poopy diaper that can unintentionally make them feel shame or embarrassment. Societal expectations are pretty much that pooping isn't something you talk about—it is something to be kept private. And kids pick up on that from a very young age when they see us going into the bathroom and closing the door when we ourselves need to poop, or making comments about how stinky or messy or gross poop can be. To help reverse that so they feel more comfortable with the idea of pooping in general—eventually of pooping on the potty—try to shift your language. Clinical trial findings published in 2003[7] showed that parents who eliminated negative terms for feces and offered praise for pooping, shortened the overall amount of time for their child to potty train by about 3 months. So starting right now, whenever your child poops, shift your language from, "Pee-eew! Let's get you out of that stinky dirty diaper!" to, "Whoa that was a big poop! I bet your belly feels so much better now!" This will help your child stop hiding when they need to poop so they can become more

41

comfortable doing it on the potty or asking for help when they need to go. The goal here is to get your child to learn that pooping is a normal, healthy part of life.

Here are some sample scripts of what you can say to shift your child's mindset and encourage curiosity about pooping:

> *"When you eat, your body keeps what it needs and the rest turns into poop! When your body tells you it's time to poop, your tummy might feel a little full and even uncomfortable. Once you let the poop out in your diaper or the potty, your tummy will feel so much better!"*

> *"Everybody poops! Mommy, Daddy, baby brother, even animals! It's what keeps our body healthy!"*

> *"Poop is something we make inside our body. In order to make room for more food, we have to let the poop come out!"*

> *"Poop can actually be really interesting! Let's put your poop into the potty so we can check it out together."*

> *"Pooping on the potty might seem scary at first because you've never done it before. What questions do you have?"*

Purposeful Play

I always say that playfulness is a child's love language, and it is scientifically proven to be one of the most effective ways in which they learn. So any way you can incorporate play into the learning process is going to be hugely beneficial and, most likely, very well received by your child. The easiest way to do this during the potty learning process is by using a drink-and-wet doll. Easily found in most big box stores or online, a drink-and-wet doll usually comes with a bottle and a small potty. You put water into the doll using the bottle, and then the doll wets. If your child is playing with the doll and some of the water makes it into the potty, be sure to really celebrate the doll's success! Not only does this help your child learn the mechanics of the body —

as in, when liquid goes in, it makes pee come out—but it also allows them to see that using the potty can be fun and that the doll receives a really positive response, so they'll be more likely to want to try, too. Additionally, and this is huge—it gives your child a certain level of control over the process. This roleplay can be refreshing for them as they become the teachers for a change, instead of the ones being taught!

As your child actually starts potty training, they can have the doll or toy as their "potty buddy"—someone or something that accompanies them to the potty every time they need to go. Then they won't feel so isolated as they are going through this change.

Modeling

As I already discussed, the bathroom can be a scary environment for your child, especially if they have certain sensory aversions or are re-sistant to change and transition. Modeling toileting behaviors is one of the best places to start teaching your child about what happens in the bathroom and why. Each time you use the bathroom throughout the day, invite your child along. Say, "Oh, Mommy's body is telling her it's time to go potty!" and ask them to keep you company, tell you a story, or sing you a song while you sit. While you're in the bathroom, talk through the different steps. As you do this a few times, you can start involving your child more and ask them what step comes next. "I just finished putting my pee in the potty. What happens next?" See if they are able to participate by handing you some toilet paper, help-ing to flush, or pumping some soap into your hands. All of this is not only teaching them the steps of using the potty, but it is getting them comfortable with being in the bathroom environment.

Take it a step further if your child seems comfortable and place a small floor potty in the bathroom next to or across from the toilet. Invite your child to sit while you're sitting and see if they want to mirror your actions, even if they just sit fully clothed for now. Alternatively, you can offer them a turn to sit on the toilet after you've gone. Just remember that for the time being, we are following their lead, so if they say "no," don't push it any further; simply say, "Okay, maybe next time."

Introducing the Potty

Another thing to check off your list before even thinking about making the move away from diapers is to familiarize your child with the potty and normalize the concept. This process might take a little more time and patience for your family, but it's all about making your child feel comfortable in order to minimize resistance as you officially begin potty training.

Children with disabilities often struggle with change, and this is perfectly natural. New routines can be overwhelming, so your child might feel anxious about stepping out of their comfort zone for any number of reasons. One of the best ways to help them adjust is by introducing the potty in a low-pressure, positive way. Start by talking about the potty and what it's for in ways that make sense to your child. This might include letting them see and explore the potty at their own pace, even allowing them to sit with their clothes on to start out, if that puts them at ease.

Reading stories or watching videos about potty training are some other fun ways to help your child learn about the potty without it feeling like a chore. I dive into this and other visually-based preparatory activities in more detail in Chapter 8. Introducing the potty without putting pressure on your child to perform will help the potty feel safe and familiar when it's time to say goodbye to diapers. Remember, potty training isn't just about getting pee and poop into the potty. It is a complex set of combined skills, allowing progress to present itself in a variety of ways.

As you are first introducing the potty to your child, keep your sessions short and positive. If your child shows signs of resistance or anxiety, it's okay to take a step back and try again later; try to follow their lead for now. Low-pressure activities like playing near the potty, having potty-related toys, or simply discussing the process casually can help ease their anxiety. Every child is different, and what works for one might not work for another. Patience, encouragement, and a bit of creativity can go a long way in making potty training a smooth transition for your child.

Standing Diaper Changes

Another helpful way to start introducing the idea of potty training is by changing your child's diaper while standing up in the bathroom. Of course, not all children with disabilities will have this option in their toolkit, so it's important to plan for what will work best for your child. But this simple change of scenery can begin to connect the concept of bodily functions with the bathroom environment, setting the stage for using the potty. While standing, you can talk to your child about the bathroom and the potty, reinforcing the idea that this is where we go to take care of business. Plus, it's a great opportunity to make diaper changes feel less intimate. Some children really crave the connection they get with their caregiver while laying down to have their diaper changed, so if that goes away, it can actually motivate some children to want to use the potty instead. Encourage your child to participate in the clean up and changing process when they are able to, such as throwing the wipe away or pulling on the clean pair of disposable training pants, and this can further empower them to take the next step of actually using the potty!

It can also be beneficial to empty the contents of a poopy diaper into the toilet. This small but powerful action reinforces the idea that poop belongs in the potty, even if your child isn't quite ready yet to do it themselves. It gives them visual and hands-on guidance in a way that feels natural and not too overwhelming, since you are already in the bathroom anyway. Remember, every child is different, and the goal is to find strategies that feel supportive and manageable for both of you as you start this process.

The Countdown

In most cases, children handle transitions better when they are given some advance notice. For example, when they have been playing at the playground and it's now time to leave, if you simply tell them "Come on, play time over, we have to go right now!" you're bound to be met with a lot more resistance, if not a full on meltdown, than if you were to say, "It's almost time for us to go. Please choose two more things to do, and then we will get in the car." With the second scenario, you kept them involved. Then when their two things are done and you say, "That was the last thing, now it's time to go!" there might still be some resistance, but you *did* give them fair warning and their reaction will likely be smaller.

The same concept applies to potty training! If you were to wake up one random morning and decide to get rid of the diapers, your child's defenses will naturally go up, resulting in a lot of pushback along the way. However, if you give them some advance notice that things are going to be changing, they'll be able to mentally prepare. The countdown strategy is great and effective for children of all ages and abilities!

In many cases, potty training is something that will happen gradually over time. Your child may be using the potty sometimes and be in diapers other times. Your child may be in underwear during the day, but still wearing diapers for nighttime, naps, school, or car rides. But generally, when your child is showing enough progress and you are feeling confident and ready to make the final transition to being diaper free, you can decide on a "hard stop" for diapers, depending on what feels right for your family. This provides your child with clearly defined expectations to use the potty for peeing and pooping from then onward and removes any confusion of having occasional access to diapers or disposable training pants.

Since saying goodbye to diapers is a bigger transition than leaving the playground, I typically recommend taking between three to five days to start your countdown. Young kids or children with certain disabilities might not be able to comprehend the concept of time per se, so try something more visual. You can create a paper chain and tear off a link each night before bed, you can print a calendar and "x" off the days each morning, or you can have a stack of diapers in the bathroom representing the number of days that are left. As the chain is shortened, the boxes are marked off, or the diaper stack dwindles, it is a great visual representation that the change is coming so that again, they aren't blindsided.

This all gives you some opportunity to talk to your child and prepare them for how things will be a little different. Use that opportunity to build up their confidence and empower them. Also use the opportunity to allow them to ask questions or work through any feelings of hesitation or fear. Keep in mind that you have to be ready to commit at the end of this countdown period. Because not only are you preparing them for the change, but also you are setting a clear boundary for the new expectation of using the potty. Try to mentally prepare *yourself* to stick with that boundary as much as possible as well.

Preparing Your Home

It's no secret that potty training is messy business, but there are steps you can take in advance to keep your stress over that mess at bay. Accidents are going to be part of the learning process, especially in the early stages, so be sure to roll up any area rugs, and if you have carpet in most of your house, you might want to consider picking up a pack of disposable puppy pee pads for lining the floor. That way if there's an accident, you can just toss out the affected pad and replace it with a new one. You can also use them to protect couches or other furniture, or to line your child's high chair, stroller, or wheelchair. The only place I can't recommend using them is in the car seat. Since they aren't designed for that purpose, they have the potential to compromise the car seat's safety. Alternatively, you can purchase manufacturer-specific waterproof car seat liners for those travel worries. Be sure to look for those that have been crash tested!

Another thing you'll want to protect is your child's mattress. Waterproof mattress covers are a must-have during potty training. You can get disposable or reusable ones depending on what you prefer, or those that lay on the top surface of the mattress versus slipping over the entire mattress. These are also great to use to protect couches or other furniture. It may be tempting to go for the cheapest option available, especially considering the work it'll be doing, but buyer beware—many of the cheaper mattress covers can contain harmful chemicals or toxins. Avoid those that contain PVC, which is a known human carcinogen, and/or phthalates, which can also be very dangerous to young kids and give off strong odors. Try to opt for products with natural or organic materials instead. If the material it's made from isn't listed, that would be a red flag to go with something else!

It's safe to assume that you'll be doing your fair share of clean up when your child is without diapers at first, so it can be extremely helpful to have a little cleaning caddy at the ready with paper towels, your favorite cleaning spray or stain remover (catching messes early prevents dried in stains!), and an old plastic shopping bag or trash bag for quick disposal of your trash, or to transport wet or soiled items to the laundry room.

After you officially ditch diapers, there might be instances where your child needs to use the potty during sleep times—either naps or overnight, even if you decide to keep them in disposable training pants or diapers for sleep. To help preserve sleep and get everyone back to bed as quickly as possible, I recommend having a little "potty station" in their room. This basically just looks like a towel or puppy pee pad on the floor near their crib or bed with a small floor potty on top, along with a roll of toilet paper and a few pairs of clean clothes and sheets in case of an accident. The station should be dimly lit with a nightlight or a small tap light so you don't have to turn on the lights in the room and completely awaken your child for them to use the potty. This can make it convenient and easy to use the potty and get right back to sleep. Preparing your child and your home for potty training doesn't have to be a stressful process.

The strategies we've talked about are just a few options to keep in your toolkit, and you can use them whenever it feels right for your child's unique situation. As I keep emphasizing, there is no one-size-fits-all approach, so feel free to experiment and adjust as needed. The most important thing is that you're laying a solid foundation of connection, understanding, and support, all while making the process feel manageable and fun. As you move forward, remember to be flexible and patient with both your child and yourself. Trust that you'll find what works best for your family!

Courtney and James: When Medical Needs Reprioritize Potty Training

James is in third grade as I'm writing this, so it's hard to remember all the way back to when we started potty training, which was right before he entered preschool six years ago. I must have felt the pressure then to start, so we tried going pants-free for quicker trips to the bathroom but didn't really get anywhere. I was overwhelmed with the process and how many messes I was finding around the house, having more laundry than I could keep up with. We just couldn't live that way; it wasn't fair to anyone.

James was in preschool for only two months when he was diagnosed with leukemia, which culminated in a bone marrow transplant that saved his life. His school at the time, which was well-accustomed to helping students with disabilities potty train, had developed a training plan for him. However, once he was diagnosed, getting out of diapers was no longer on our radar. About a year and a half later, in late January 2020, James returned to school, but before the potty training plan could be reimplemented, the world shut down for COVID-19. Whatever support we might have had access to—therapists, school staff—was suddenly out of reach.

We tried going pants-free again but were faced with the same challenges we had experienced two years before, so I was relieved when I found guidance online from a potty training expert who worked specifically with the disability community who suggested placing your child in regular underwear and then pulling rubber pants over. The theory was that the child would feel an accident, but it was contained,

50

saving the parent the distress over cleaning up day in and day out. Another bit of advice that I received was to put little training potties throughout the house, which was great because one of our biggest challenges early on was getting James to actually go into the bathroom. So again, I felt relief and validation in meeting my child where he was and providing him what he actually needed. For the first time, I really thought that we could do this.

After the starts and stops of potty training throughout preschool, and once the kids had returned to school full-time postpandemic, I met a mom at an ELM event (of all places!) who shared her experience with a potty trainer for her own child years prior. The trainer traditionally went into families' homes for one very intense week, but because she wasn't local to the area, we worked with her virtually. Probably understanding that what she did in people's homes wasn't easily replicated by parents via video chats, she revised her formula to training sessions that involved a pretty structured period of what we lovingly referred to as "naked time."

The trainer disagreed vehemently with both rubber pants over underwear and placing potties around the house, which at first was really discouraging because at different times before this I'd found myself empowered by each of these strategies. She also didn't love that James stood up to pee (she preferred boys sitting down), but she agreed to continue letting him go this way because he was successful with it. We made the bathroom inviting with some fun lights. We also made sure the toilet was accessible for him, so keeping the seat up and having a clear path were both very important.

I discovered with James that we couldn't play on the floor because it was too much effort and energy to get up off the floor and make it to the toilet in time. So, I set up a table right outside the bathroom, which meant fewer barriers for him to get to the potty, plus I could be more aware of his signs. If I noticed any indication from him, I'd run him to the bathroom by telling him, "You're showing me a sign that you have to go!" Close proximity and no pants made a big difference. I found it hard sometimes to get him to stand up from the table and move to the bathroom, and in those cases I would drag the chair to the bathroom door with him still sitting on it, and then he'd be more willing to stand up and go to the potty.

The problem with this method was that I was supposed to be sitting there actively during our training segments, watching his signs until he had to use the bathroom, which was time consuming and unsustainable. If I noticed a sign, even just a physical one like a little bubble of pee coming out, I would treat it as him initiating—fake it 'til you make it! A less obvious sign would be when he was touching himself, and I took that as a sign, too.

The trainer's big thing with pee was *initiate, initiate, initiate*. She was always pointing out how often we were prompting James to go, even when we didn't realize we were, but we didn't really feel like he felt it enough to initiate on his own. We used a lot of praise as reinforcement when he'd pee, which was actually more rewarding and natural than a sticker chart we'd previously phased out. We also began reinforcing initiating with "big" prizes and reinforcing staying dry all day and pooping in the potty with "huge" prizes. Both of these sets of prizes were actually pretty small, but they were impactful to James and thereby reinforcing.

Having made so much progress with pee, we decided to focus on poop training. The trainer helped us identify that poop was the culprit holding him back from wearing underwear. He was only occasionally wet with pee but always pooped in his diaper. Whereas the trainer believed in initiation for peeing, she was okay with prompting for poop. She shared her protocol with us, which was a recommended structured period between dinner and bedtime. When I shared this with my husband, I thought, "We don't have any extra second of time! How are we going to do this?" He made the thoughtful suggestion that we wait until summer—it was fall at this time—but I just didn't think

52

it was fair to James to have him wait any longer for this support.

In addition to having Down syndrome and low muscle tone, James has a swallowing disorder that requires most of his nutrition come from a gastronomy tube, which is surgically implanted in his abdomen. He had been a pretty regular pooper up to this point, which I attribute to his vegetarian diet, but when the tube feeds started, there was suddenly no predictability in when or how often he would go.

So to accommodate this new protocol, I arranged to get home early from work for two straight weeks so that I could shift our entire afternoon/evening schedule up—everything else we had to do was temporarily suspended. After dinner, we waited about a half hour and then went right outside the bathroom to a table set up similarly to our earlier "naked time." He'd have to sit down on the potty to try, never longer than for about three minutes, and I'd help him through the physical motions of pooping. After a certain period of time, we'd go back to try again. Between attempts, we'd do "poop exercises"—squats, jumps on the trampoline! If he wasn't able to go, then we would give him "poop help" with glycerin suppositories. We'd distract him with a quick video and very soon after he would need a hug and the poop just all poured out. We'd super celebrate and play, "Celebrate good times, come on!" (Now when he hears that song, even if he hasn't gone potty and is nowhere near a bathroom, he cheers for himself, "Yay! I just did poop on the potty!!" which recently happened on the dance floor at my niece's graduation party!)

This went on for two weeks and then I just couldn't take any more time off so we did pieces of it whenever we could fit it in. I felt guilty and like I was impeding his progress, then little by little he would have moments when he was standing to pee, notice he had to poop, and would say "poop!" and we'd quickly turn him around to sit down. Poop in the potty earned him some pretty big prizes! Now he has the skill of pooping on the potty and just needs to generalize it and be more consistent.

It was a little scary to move totally over to undies, but he's doing it! We've incorporated specialty leak control underwear, which look and feel like regular underwear but do a great job containing accidents, which James still has from time to time. Other days we double up on regular underwear for added absorbency, and at home he's usually in a single pair of underwear so that we can support him as he acquires the skill of initiating.

I feel more hopeful these days, like becoming fully potty trained is possible now, that we can actually accomplish this. He's come so far! And the extra time he has had at the school nurse for his tube feeds has worked in our favor because he is now pooping in the nurse's bathroom almost every morning, Monday through Friday! I'm considering bringing him for visits over the summer to keep the successes coming!

Chapter 5: Disability Factors and Considerations

As a pediatric occupational therapist, this chapter has my stamp of approval! That impact potty training for children with disabilities, while still remembering that every child is different, regardless of a diagnosis. - Lora Jackle, OTR/L

When we started framing out this book, we considered having chapters for specific disabilities. Through our combined experiences with potty training and the disability community, however, we realized that a better approach would be breaking out the various factors that impact potty training children with disabilities. Most importantly, we all know that no child is the same, whether they have a disability or not. Down syndrome does not guarantee you certain outcomes, nor does autism, cerebral palsy or the countless rare disabilities. Sometimes these labels lead us to troubleshooting things that don't even apply to our children, neither now nor ever! You may have even picked up this book because your child has low muscle tone, communication delays, or sensory sensitivities without a specific disability diagnosis. We hope that this chapter can help you navigate some of the common factors that challenge potty training, in a way that resonates with your experiences with your unique child.

Potty training is a complex developmental milestone on its own, even before adding in a disability diagnosis that might include traits such as sensory issues or communication delays. But by learning about the potential impacts these factors might have on your journey, you can keep the following analyses in mind as you are developing your strategy and navigating the process of potty training your child. In fact, there are a lot of characteristics to consider that you may have never even associated with potty training before.

Let's cover some of the most common associated traits that children with various disabilities display so you can gain some insight into how your potty training experience might look. As you continue reading, you will also find tips, recommendations, and tools relating to many of these characteristics that can help to improve and adapt your experience.

Considerations for Major Disability Types

Intellectual Disabilities

Examples: Down Syndrome, Fragile X Syndrome, Cerebral Palsy, Fetal Alcohol Syndrome, Autism Spectrum Disorder

Possible challenges:

- Physical versus cognitive readiness could come at different times. Your child might be able to physically execute on what they are able to understand. Alternatively, one of these two skills may come before the other: your child might be able to learn about the steps and purpose of potty training well before you attempt to remove diapers. Advancing learning in ways that work for them will make the process easier when the timing is right for them to do it themselves!
- Sensory sensitivities might upstage readiness. What might come across as resistance or not being ready for potty training could simply be a sensory challenge. Adapting the bathroom environment so your child feels comfortable and safe can make the process more enjoyable and progress more smoothly.
- Certain diagnoses may be accompanied by additional physical symptoms that aren't revealed until potty training begins. For example, hypotonia or low muscle tone can make bladder and bowel control and coordination more challenging.

Strategies that will work:

- Gradual introduction to potty training
- Allow time for practice and preparation before removing diapers
- Schedule potty times
- Prompt potty visits
- Break the process down into smaller, more manageable steps
- Visual supports to supplement language and communication
- Use rewards and reinforcers
- Ongoing parent/caregiver support for some aspects of toileting

Developmental Disabilities

Examples: Autism Spectrum Disorder, ADHD, Down Syndrome, Fetal Alcohol Syndrome

Possible challenges:

- Your child may not be socially motivated to use the toilet, resulting in potty training initiation later than for their peers.
- Your child likely struggles with transitions, making preparation for potty training and advance notice of the upcoming changes extra important.
- Sensory sensitivities can play a role in potty training. Take time to consider your child's aversions or preferences and adapt the bathroom environment accordingly, allowing them to feel comfortable and relaxed.
- Your child may be a selective eater, which is very common with this type of diagnosis. And the truth is, it's not that they are selective because they are difficult, but they may have dietary limitations, aversions to certain textures or tastes, or only eat preferred foods due to sensory processing needs. This type of eating can lead to constipation or poor gut health, so be sure to speak with your child's doctor or a dietitian who can offer solutions.

- This type of diagnosis may also be accompanied by physical symptoms, such as muscle weakness or motor challenges, making bladder and bowel control/coordination more challenging. Joint pain may occur, which could make sitting on the toilet for longer periods of time uncomfortable. Skin issues may cause bruising from all the hard surfaces in the bathroom.
- Your child may struggle with urge recognition and/or stopping activities to use the bathroom more than a typically developing child due to trouble with prefrontal cortex functions, such as planning, decision making, self-control, or task completion. This can lead to more accidents during the learning process.
- Communication challenges can lead to struggles with following directions or self-initiation. However, even if your child is nonverbal, they are capable of learning how to use the potty with the right tools in place.

Strategies that will work:

- Play-based approach
- Use rewards and reinforcers
- Provide age- and developmentally appropriate choices so your child can feel in control
- Focus on attainable goals based on your child's unique development and needs
- Use consistency; avoid added transitions, like small potty chairs or spending time naked before moving to underwear
- Communication support
- Visual aids

Physical Disabilities

Examples: Cerebral Palsy, Muscular Dystrophy, Spina Bifida

Possible challenges:

- To master all steps of the process, potty training a child with a physical disability often requires a team, including parents, caregivers, doctors, physical therapists, occupational therapists, and other specialists.
- Physical symptoms may add challenges with muscle weakness or tightness, joint pain, motor function, and coordinating large muscle groups, making both accessing the toilet and voiding their bladder and bowels at controlled times more difficult.
- If your child needs assistance getting onto the toilet, it could lead to more accidents, depending on how quickly you are able to respond to their needs.
- Communication might be limited, making self-initiation difficult.
- Because the bathroom environment may need to be adapted with certain equipment to make using the toilet safer and easier for your child, using a public toilet may be more of a challenge if these adaptations aren't readily available.
- Goals and definitions of progress and success might need to be modified. Potty training for your child might not look like being diaper free, but instead, your child being able to use the toilet at certain times throughout the day so their diaper stays dry or mostly dry. Or it may be that they have their bowel movements in the toilet while still wearing diapers the rest of the time. (Every situation is different, so keep your expectations realistic and manageable for both you and your child!)

Strategies that will work:

- If your child will need support getting onto the toilet, consider adaptive equipment that might make the process easier for you both.
- Portable equipment, foldable stools, foldable potty seats with handles (support on the go)
- Plan for safety and stability while using the toilet.
- An individualized approach will likely be required based on your child's unique needs and abilities.
- Routine toilet visits may be easier than relying on self-initiation alone.
- Use of visual and communication aids can help your child understand the process and communicate their needs or preferences about the potty.
- Use rewards and reinforcers.

Elements of Different Disabilities and the Potential Impact on Potty Training

Like we touched on above, your child's disability unfortunately does not come with a manual or easy-to-follow roadmap. There are many factors that can impact potty training, and the tools in your toolkit likely won't look the same as another parent navigating the same disability. This section is where we encourage you to get out your highlighter, take some notes, and read with a keen eye for what "sounds like" your child. This is where you'll start to build your strategies based on the factors that could be impacting your child. You may even want to discuss with your care team (more on who is best for which factors toward the end of this chapter!) and start to work some of these strategies into therapy, school routines, etc.

Impairments

Vision. If your child has a visual impairment, they may struggle with finding the potty or bathroom, especially in an unfamiliar space. Understanding the purpose of the toilet, undressing, or wiping may mean you will need to provide hands-on assistance, accurate verbal descriptions, and/or tactile cues to help them safely and effectively navigate the bathroom environment. Try using high contrast tools to help identify visual boundaries, like colored tape.

Hearing. If your child has a hearing impairment, it can impact their communication and ability to understand instructions, which could require some adaptation. Children with hearing impairments will likely struggle to comprehend verbal instructions or cues related to using the toilet. You may need to equip your child with visual supports and demonstrations, as well as ways to communicate from both a receptive and expressive standpoint. Teaching the proper sign language for words like "potty," "poop," or "all done," or adding them to their AAC device, or using single-pictorial representations in common places, will give your child more confidence during the process.

Sensory input or processing. Sensory processing disorders span across many diagnoses and can significantly impact potty training by affecting a child's sensory experiences and responses to stimuli. Some children may have sensory aversions, such as to the loud sound of a toilet flushing or a hand dryer, to the bright lights in the bathroom, or to the way their underwear's elastic waistband feels on their skin. Other children may be sensory seekers and may find satisfaction in tactile inputs, like handling their feces or not minding a wet or soiled diaper. Additionally, children who struggle with sensory issues may have a hard time with understanding their body's signals for when they need to use the bathroom, making urge recognition more difficult. Identifying these sensory needs before starting the process can help you create a plan for your child to accommodate their specific preferences, make the bathroom a more inviting space, and avoid things that could cause setbacks in their learning.

Speech or language. Children with speech, language, or communication delays may face challenges with potty training due to difficulties in understanding and expressing their needs. I often find that children who are delayed with speech or communication tend to be delayed with potty training as well. These delays can hinder their ability to communicate when they need to use the bathroom or understand instructions related to potty training. Additionally, they may struggle to articulate their feelings or sensations associated with the urge to go, making it harder for you to recognize their cues.

Interestingly enough, there is a complex connection between the mouth and the pelvic floor. Therefore, problems that may contribute to your child's speech delay could also contribute to complications during potty training. For example, tethered oral tissues (TOTs), more commonly referred to as lip, tongue, or cheek tie, may cause additional pull or tightness to the pelvic floor because they are ultimately connected with the same web of fascia. This has the potential to make a child more prone to daytime pee accidents, bedwetting, or constipation.

Providing clear, simple language, using visual aids, and establishing consistent routines can help support your child in overcoming communication barriers and developing the necessary skills for successful potty training. We'll be getting into this in more detail in the coming chapters.

Proprioception. Proprioception is a sense that can be impacted by various disabilities. Just like other senses, it plays a crucial role in potty training as it involves the body's awareness of its own movements and positioning in space. Proprioception differences can also equate to issues with tolerance of clothing changes. Children rely on proprioceptive feedback to understand how to sit properly on the toilet, coordinate their muscles for bowel and bladder control, and adjust their posture during the process. Proper proprioceptive input helps children develop the motor skills necessary for using the toilet independently. For example, proprioceptive input informs them about the pressure needed to push or relax their muscles to push out poop effectively. Providing opportunities for your child to practice sitting on the toilet, supporting them in finding a comfortable position, and offering feedback on body awareness can all contribute to successful potty training by enhancing proprioceptive development.

Interoception. Interoception, or the awareness of internal bodily sensations, is an important part of potty training because it is needed to help children recognize and respond to the signals from their bladder and bowels. Urges such as the need to pee or poop are detected through interoceptive cues, just like feeling hunger, pain, or changes in temperature. Children who are attuned to these signals can understand when they need to use the toilet and respond accordingly. However, difficulties in interoception can lead to challenges in recognizing and interpreting these bodily cues, resulting in accidents or delays in self-initiation. Therefore, promoting interoceptive awareness through sensory activities, mindfulness practices, and verbal reinforcement may be necessary if your child struggles with this sense. It's important to think about how your child lets you know about other internal cues, like hunger, pain, thirst, etc., and lean on that for communication about potty training.

Retained Primitive Reflexes. Retained primitive reflexes, or RPRs, are involuntary, automatic movements that a child develops in utero and typically grows out of within their first few months, but are retained into childhood when their development is disrupted in some way. This could be as a result of birth trauma, injury, illness, or some other cause. Certain RPRs can directly impact potty training. For example, the Spinal Galant Reflex causes a baby to curve or wiggle their hips when their lower back is stroked near the spine. This reflex is there to eventually aid in developing the range of motion needed in the hips for crawling and walking and typically fades when a baby is between 3 to 9 months old. When this reflex is retained, it can trigger a child's bladder to void when the lower back is touched, making a simple thing like sitting in a chair or wearing a tighter waistband a problem for potty progress.

Likewise, a retained Moro reflex can make potty training particularly challenging, especially when it comes to sitting on the toilet. The Moro reflex, also known as the startle reflex, is a natural response to sudden changes in position or sensations of falling. If this reflex is retained into early childhood, it can cause a feeling of gravitational instability, which can be frightening for some children. While perched on the toilet, they may feel like they are going to fall off, or they might experience the sensation of actually falling, which can make the whole process feel unsettling and unsafe. To help alleviate this, adaptive equipment can be incredibly beneficial. A seat insert with back support, along with handles for stability, can give the child more support at the hips, in combination with a step stool for foot support, allowing them to feel more secure and grounded while sitting.

There are simple tests that can be done to determine whether your child has any RPRs, allowing their therapy team to implement integrative exercises.

Activity Limitation

Hypotonia. Hypotonia, or low muscle tone, is a condition that can stand alone or accompany many different disabilities. Since a large part of potty training involves muscle control, it can significantly impact potty training by affecting your child's ability to hold their bladder and bowel muscles at the proper times, leading to frequent accidents or even incontinence. Children with hypotonia may also struggle to maintain proper posture while sitting on the toilet or lack the strength to support themselves during the process. You may need to provide them with additional support, such as using adaptive equipment, like step stools or toilet seats with handles or physically assisting them with positioning. Physical therapy that focuses on the core and pelvic floor can also help improve muscle tone and strength, making bladder and bowel control more achievable.

Hypertonia. The opposite of hypotonia, hypertonia is characterized by increased muscle tone and stiffness. This can also pose challenges during potty training due to difficulties in muscle coordination and control. Children with hypertonia can experience muscle contractions or spasming and may struggle to relax the muscles needed to release their bladder and bowels, ultimately leading to difficulties with peeing and pooping. This will often lead to issues with constipation that require intervention, like using the fiber supplement HyFiber® for Kids (learn more about why we love them in Chapter 13). These children may also struggle with posture or finding a comfortable position on the toilet. If this applies to your child, you can help by adapting the bathroom environment to accommodate their specific needs and implementing strategies to promote relaxation. Physical or occupational therapists with specific knowledge of and experience with the pelvic floor can provide exercises to relax these muscles, allowing for better coordination.

Independence/dependence with movement. If your child lacks independence with movement, they will likely encounter difficulties using the bathroom due to limitations in their mobility and coordination. Without the ability to move freely, they may struggle to access the bathroom, reach the toilet, adjust their clothing, or assume the necessary posture for peeing and pooping. Additionally, they may rely heavily on you or a caregiver for help with transferring to and from the toilet and dressing and undressing, which can cause them to feel a lack of autonomy and privacy. They might also have a limited ability to respond quickly to the urge to use the bathroom, increasing the likelihood of accidents. Fostering independence through mobility aids and adaptive equipment, scheduling bathroom visits, and physical therapy interventions can be helpful to empower your child to navigate potty training more effectively.
Participation Restrictions

Self-initiation. Self-initiation is one of those things that all parents strive for as they tackle potty training because it means your child is able to recognize their urges and then let you know, so you're not always anticipating an accident. But for children with disabilities, it might take longer to learn this skill, if they are ever able to attain it at all. Sensory processing difficulties, neurological impairments, or developmental delays can significantly impair interoception and communication skills, making it more challenging for some kids to express their needs or intentions effectively. Additionally, certain medical conditions or physical limitations may further hinder their ability to recognize or convey signals related to using the potty. As a result, they may require ongoing assistance or rely on a structured schedule to help them manage their bathroom needs. A toileting schedule provides consistency and predictability, allowing you and other caregivers to anticipate and prompt bathroom visits at regular intervals. Providing ongoing assistance ensures that your child receives the support needed to maintain hygiene and prevent accidents so they can navigate potty training with both dignity and comfort. Giving your child control with something like a potty watch can help them transition from having to be prompted to self-initiation. This may give them a repetitive tool to start to let you know when they have to go.

Motor skill support. Fine or gross motor skill delays can impact the potty training process as well. Children who are delayed in their gross motor skills may struggle with executing some or all of the physical movements involved in using the potty. These children may lack the muscle strength and coordination needed to control their bladder and bowel movements or to respond quickly to the urge to use the bathroom. Children who have fine motor skill delay may struggle with the more intricate tasks associated with potty training, such as manipulating clothing, flushing, wiping, and washing their hands independently. In both cases, your child may need extra assistance or adaptive equipment, as well as occupational or physical therapy to help them with the potty training process.

Full potty independence. Some children with disabilities never become fully independent with potty use, depending on the nature and severity of their condition, and if this might be your path, know you aren't alone. Certain disabilities affect cognitive, physical, or sensory abilities to such an extent that mastering the skills required for independent bathroom use becomes too challenging for your child, or sometimes for you as well. There are a lot of factors that can contribute to ongoing difficulties with potty training and it's always important to weigh your own desires and goals for your child with their ultimate happiness and well-being. If using the potty adds too much stress or is taking a toll on your relationship with your child, that could be a sign that the timing isn't right, or that other goals should be prioritized, at least temporarily. In these types of cases, you can focus on alternative strategies, such as promoting partial independence or simply maximizing comfort and hygiene, to support your child overall, while acknowledging and respecting their individual abilities and limitations. It's all about embracing your own unique journey and realizing that success and progress look different for everyone.

Physical Therapist Considerations for Potty Training

By Brittany Steindl, DPT, BLS Physical Therapy
Pediatric Physical Therapist

Body Posture and Alignment	Optimal body posture can significantly impact the ease of passing a bowel movement. Encouraging a slight forward-leaning posture with knees above the hips promotes a relaxed position for the pelvic floor muscles, which helps to reduce straining.
Using a Footstool	A footstool like a Squatty Potty® aligns a child's body in a natural squat position, which can improve the effectiveness of bowel movements. This position straightens the rectum and supports the abdominal muscles, making it easier to pass stool without strain.
Deep Squat Exercises	Practicing deep squats can strengthen the muscles around the abdomen and pelvis, helping the child to gain more control. A daily routine of deep squats—holding each squat for a few seconds—can engage these muscles, improving bowel movement control and reducing constipation.
Core Strengthening Exercises	Core exercises, like bridges, sit-ups, and gentle twists, are helpful for building the muscles needed for effective bowel movements. Stronger core muscles support better intra-abdominal pressure, which assists in easier passing of stools.
Consistency and Routine	A regular toilet schedule can provide children with sensory or motor planning difficulties with predictable structure, making the process less stressful. Encourage sitting on the toilet at the same time each day, particularly after meals, to take advantage of natural digestive reflexes.
Positive Reinforcement and Visual Supports	Use visual schedules or reward charts to support children who need predictability. Clear visual steps can break down each stage of the toilet routine, while rewards for attempts and successes can reinforce the new habit positively.
Breathing Techniques	Encourage deep breathing exercises to help relax the abdominal muscles and pelvic floor, reducing the tension that can make bowel movements more difficult. Practicing this during seated potty times can help the child feel more relaxed.

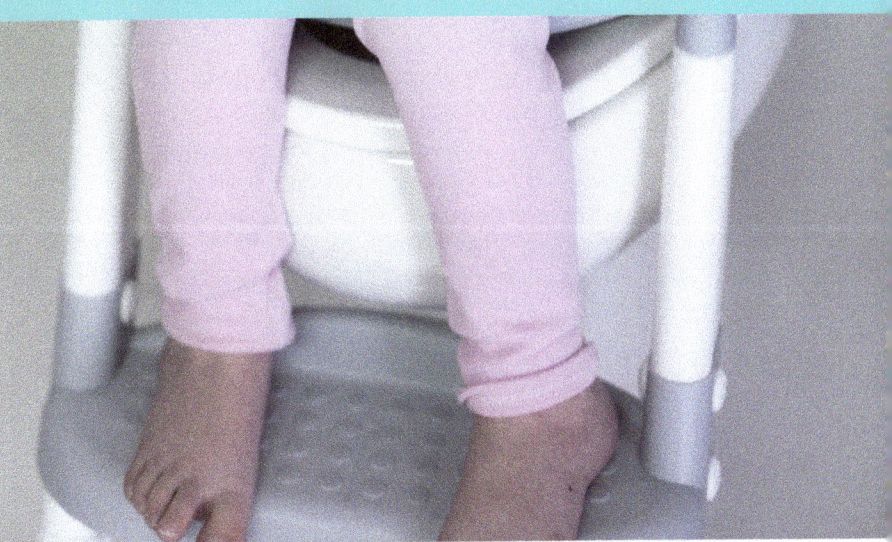

POTTY LIKE A PRO

Implementation

Chapter 6:
Potty Training Supplies

Choosing the right potty training supplies is an important step in setting your child up for success. In this chapter, we'll explore how to select the best potty, underwear, and other helpful tools that will make the potty training process smoother and more comfortable for your child. Whether your child has specific needs or preferences, finding the right supplies can help them feel empowered, confident, and ready to take on this new milestone. Let's dive into how to make these choices, with both practicality and your child's unique needs in mind.

Choosing a Floor Potty or the Toilet

When it comes to potty training, choosing between a small floor potty and the regular toilet can feel like a big decision. Each option has its benefits, and the right choice really depends on your child's unique needs and preferences. But there are so many different options out there that it can sometimes be confusing or overwhelming as to which one is best. Should you go with perhaps the most obvious choice and get the small floor potty? Or is it better to skip that step and go straight to the toilet since that's the end goal anyway? My expert opinion is that it depends on a lot of different factors. In most cases, I recommend starting out with a combination of both so you can take advantage of the benefits of both! But in reality, there is no right or wrong answer as long as you are choosing something that your child and your family is comfortable with. Eventually moving away from diapers is what's most important! Let's break down the differences and help you make the best decision for your little one.

Some of the many pros of using a floor potty include:

Convenience. It can be moved around easily and kept within arms' reach, especially for those first few days without diapers, making it much more accessible to catch a success and less inconvenient than having to stop and go all the way to the bathroom for your child. Then, when you're ready to venture out, it can be kept right in the car for easy pottying on the go.

Size. It's small. This can help take away the intimidation factor that comes along with the actual toilet. A smaller size also makes it safer and easier for your child to get onto it independently.

Posture. It gives your child great stability and foot support because it's right on the ground, almost always putting them in the ideal physical posture—that natural squat position—to easily release their bladder and bowels.

There are lots of different potty options out there, with our favorites from Jool Baby® in our product guide linked at the end of this chapter, but here are some tips when making your selection:

- White is always better than a color so it more closely resembles the toilet and is less easily confused as a toy. That said, if you have a child who is super into racecars who has been resistant to potty training in the past and they are excited to finally sit on a potty that looks like a racecar, then by all means, get that racecar potty!
- Make sure the potty is easy to clean without a bunch of nooks and crannies where pee can get stuck. Something with a removable, rinsable bowl is ideal.
- Look for something with a decent height splash guard. When kids (both boys and girls) first start peeing in the potty, the spray factor is real. Having a higher splash guard will save your floors and your sanity.

- Opt for something budget friendly. You don't necessarily need to get sucked into the higher dollar potties when it's not something your child will be using long term. Instead, go for a less expensive option and get more than one so you have one for each level of your home, or one for home and one for the car.
- While added bells and whistles like music or flushing sounds aren't necessary, they can be a way to add some fun and excitement to the process for your child. Think about what your child enjoys when selecting a potty. You can always let them decorate it with stickers or markers to personalize it even more.

Okay, now that we've covered small potties, what about starting off straight on the toilet? That has its fair share of benefits, too:

Cleanup. When your child uses the toilet, the pee and poop go straight in (most of the time at least), ready to be flushed away. There's no added cleanup like you'll have with a floor potty.

Association. The fact that the toilet is in the bathroom and stays in the bathroom can help kids who are struggling with certain aspects of potty training connect their bodily functions with the bathroom environment. This makes it easier to maintain that "for business only" type mindset—the toilet is where we pee and poop. Period. Not a TV watching seat or a snack eating seat, which can sometimes happen unintentionally with a floor potty.

Transition. By starting off with the toilet, you avoid the possibility of having to transition your child from the floor potty later on, providing consistency and preventing confusion. Not often, but sometimes, kids will become dependent on the floor potty, making toilet use much more challenging for them and possibly limiting their ability to use the toilet in places other than the home. There will be toilet access the majority of places you go, and almost never small potty access, unless you bring your own. So getting that early exposure to the toilet is beneficial for experience at home, school, restaurants, stores, airports, and more. Starting with a regular toilet is the best option to reach that end goal we're all after: potty confidence in any environment.

One size fits all. Many children with disabilities won't begin potty training until they have already grown too big for a small floor potty, so the toilet becomes the only natural choice. Just remember to provide foot support so your child can get on the potty on their own, as well as for added stability. You may also choose to fit the toilet with a seat reducer, with or without handles, if your child needs that extra physical support.

Overall, if you are starting potty training from scratch and your child still qualifies from a size perspective, then starting out with both a small floor potty option as well as giving your child plenty of exposure to and practice with the regular toilet in the bathroom is the ideal scenario. Using the small floor potty sets your child up for more successes during those first few days without diapers and while pottying on the go, but using the actual toilet sometimes is going to help them be more comfortable using one in places other than at home.

There are some cases where I would recommend skipping the small floor potty and using the toilet right off the bat. If your child already has experience with and is comfortable with the toilet, perhaps from school or daycare, for example, then you would be okay to forgo the floor potty and go for the toilet right away. Additionally, if your child has a disability that makes transitions or changes more difficult, it is best to start right away with the toilet to avoid that additional transition from floor potty to toilet, which can just end up being disruptive and confusing, potentially prolonging your entire potty training process.

Based on all of this information, when you decide to incorporate the toilet for your child's potty training, whether it be right away, or at some point later on, it will be very important to consider safety, stability, and good toileting posture. So, using a seat insert or seat reducer on top of the toilet is always a good idea for your potty learner. There are different varieties to choose from when it comes to these as well.

You might choose a super simple option, like a removable plastic potty seat, paired with a separate step stool for foot support. (Please note, you never want your child's feet to be dangling while they're

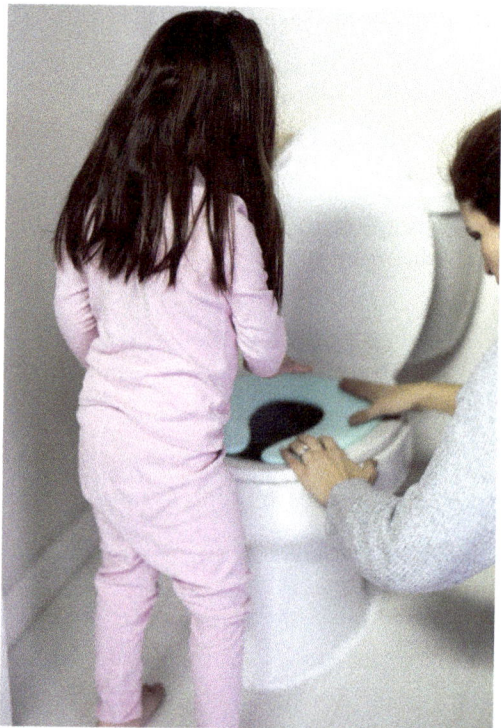

on the toilet.) Selecting one with handles is also a great idea to give your child something to hold, providing added stability, or you can ease some of their sensory aversions by selecting a seat with padding.

You can go for a larger fixture with a built-in ladder attachment. Some nice features to look for in this type of potty seat are padding, or an extra step to help your child get into that natural squat position.

You can also get something more discreet that becomes a permanent fixture in the bathroom, which is great for bathrooms that might be used by guests as well. The child-size seat is built right into the regular toilet seat and can be pulled down whenever your child needs to use the potty; just remember that your child will still need foot support for this one.

If you aren't quite sure how to decide, get your child involved in the selection process. Pull up pictures of a few options that you're okay with and then let them pick which one they like best, or take them on a shopping trip to the store to do a potty test drive. Any way you can offer choices throughout this process is a great way to help your child feel involved and in control. At the end of the day, if your child is using the floor potty, the toilet, or some combination of both, it doesn't matter, because it's all considered a huge success!

Choosing Underwear

As you are getting closer to the switch over from diapers, plan on transitioning your child straight into underwear. And selecting your child's first underwear, much like selecting their potty, is a very personal choice. You might not think there's much more to it than grabbing a few packs on your next shopping run, but there are some factors to consider when it comes to choosing the best option for your child as they make the transition from diapers to underwear for the first time.

For all children, comfort is obviously a top priority. We don't want your child to protest wearing underwear because they aren't comfortable in them. But comfort might look different for different kids. Think about any sensory sensitivities your child might have when it comes to clothing: tags, seams, or tight fitting elastics could all potentially bother a child who is new to the world of underwear. To help your child feel more excited about the transition, you can take them shopping and select some they are drawn to.

Also, avoiding briefs for boys and bikinis for girls, which tend to fit more like a diaper, and instead opting for a boxer short or boxer brief style underwear for boys or a boy short style for girls helps increase their awareness of their body's urges. Generally, lightweight breathable fabrics are ideal, and you can even go up a size from what your child would normally wear to make accidents less easily contained and therefore more uncomfortable. If your child doesn't like the way accidents feel in their new underwear, that will be a deterrent to do it again. Plus, having them fit more loosely will eventually make it easier for your child to pull them up and down without assistance from you.

Potty training underwear, which is essentially regular underwear with a thicker absorbent lining in the crotch area, might be super tempting to buy just based on the name alone; however, I would only recommend using these in certain situations. If your child has padded underwear on, first of all it is going to feel more similar to a diaper, which could potentially be confusing or send mixed signals, and secondly, the absorbency isn't going to allow them to be as aware when an accident occurs, which can hinder the learning process. However, times when it would be okay to use training underwear would be anytime that you are tempted to resort to disposable training underwear out of fear of an accident or for an added convenience factor. This may be on a longer car ride, if your commute involves public transportation, if your child is having a hard time mastering dry naps, or if your child's school, daycare, or therapy isn't quite ready for the switch to regular underwear. So, overall, they aren't really necessary, but it wouldn't hurt to have a pack on hand for those "just in case" moments.

Lucky & Me™ is a great choice for kids with sensory sensitivities because their kids' underwear and clothing is designed with comfort and durability in mind. The perfect comfy fit ensures that underwear stays in place with no riding up or sliding around so your child can focus on having fun and on daily tasks without distractions. They use soft, premium materials, like organic cotton and plush elastics, and their clothes feel amazing against sensitive skin. If your child is bothered by seams, tight elastic, or tags, Lucky & Me™ could be a good option.

Not to mention, they're built to last, retaining their shape and color even after multiple washes, which, let's face it, might happen as your child becomes a potty pro!

Adaptive Clothing

When it comes to potty training, choosing the right underwear for your child is just the beginning! There are also fantastic options for adaptive clothing specifically designed to make the process smoother for children with disabilities. For example, clothing featuring hook-and-loop closures or magnetic fastenings can make dressing and undressing much easier for kids who have fine motor skill difficulties or limited dexterity.

Look for clothes with elastic waistbands, adjustable straps, or even those without tags, as these offer extra flexibility and comfort. If your child has a mobility impairment, they might find adaptive clothing with side openings or snap closures particularly helpful, as these allow for faster and easier access during bathroom visits.

What I love most about adaptive clothing is how it promotes dignity and inclusion. By allowing children with disabilities to participate in potty activities more independently, these clothes encourage a sense of accomplishment and empowerment as they move toward greater independence. Every little step forward is a victory, and the right clothing can make all the difference in your child's potty training journey!

Potty Training Shopping List

At-Home Recommendations

- Floor potty
- Potty ladder with seat & handles
- Padded seat reducers for additional toilets
- Footstool for proper positioning
- Sensory-friendly underwear (12-15 pairs)
- Puppy pads for floors/furniture
- Flushable wipes
- Stickers and/or rewards
- Mattress protection
- Visual charts
- Potty watch
- Fiber-rich foods or supplements

SCAN FOR ALL OF OUR FAVORITE PRODUCTS!

On-The-Go Recommendations

- Travel potty for your car
- Foldable potty seat
- Toilet sensor blockers

Chapter 7:
The Bathroom Environment

For many children with disabilities, the first step in potty training success is simply feeling relaxed and at ease in the bathroom. Creating the perfect bathroom setup for potty training means keeping your child's unique needs and preferences (and apprehensions!) in mind. A few simple tweaks can make the space just right for them. Here we will talk about how to get your child more comfortable with the bathroom, how to make the space safe and accessible, and the various types of adaptive equipment that will help make the potty training process easier to manage.

Getting Comfortable with the Bathroom

As you get started, you may notice your child having some uncertainty, anxiety, or outright fear surrounding the bathroom or toilet. This isn't unusual, especially for kids with disabilities, when shifts in routine are definitely not preferred. For children who need extra time and support to feel comfortable in the bathroom, it's important to recognize that this is a normal part of the potty training process. Every child progresses at their own pace, and rushing or pushing too hard can lead to increased stress and setbacks. Allowing your child to take their time helps build a sense of control and autonomy, which will then turn into confidence and comfort during potty training.

I always recommend gradually allowing your child to gain exposure with the bathroom space in ways that make them feel comfortable and relaxed. For example, if your child is afraid to sit on the toilet, start by having them stand near the toilet while you hold their hand. Eventually they can try sitting on your lap while you sit on the toilet with the lid down, working toward feeling comfortable sitting on the toilet with their clothing still on. Allow your child to bring comforting items into the bathroom, like their favorite toy or blanket. Using positive reinforcement and a calm, patient demeanor can help alleviate fear and build your child's confidence. Also, establishing a consistent routine can provide a sense of predictability and security. Using visual schedules or social stories that outline each step of the potty training process will help your child understand what to expect and reduce anxiety about all the unknowns that come along with potty training. I will go into more detail on this in Chapter 8.

Many children, even those who are otherwise neurotypical, experience sensory sensitivities. The bathroom can be sensory overload—an environment that triggers discomfort and stress for children with unique sensory needs or sensory processing disorders due to all the bright lights, loud noises, and downright strange odors and textures. In fact, the start of potty training might be the first time you notice sensory aversions with your child. If your child does exhibit certain sensory dislikes or preferences, it's important to reconfigure the potty and bathroom space so they can feel as comfortable as possible.

If your child is easily overstimulated from a visual perspective, soft, muted colors on the walls and non-fluorescent lighting can help them relax. On the other hand, some children may prefer to have something visually stimulating, such as a colorful poster on the wall or an artificial fish tank to look at while they sit on the toilet. For auditory sensitivities, consider using a white noise machine or playing gentle music to mask any distracting sounds. Some children may even need ear muffs or noise-canceling headphones to ensure they don't get startled by some of the loud noises that can occur in the bathroom environment. A padded toilet seat or soft rug can provide comfort for kids with tactile sensitivity, as does ensuring that the bathroom is set to a comfortable temperature. Some kids may also be extra sensitive to new and different smells that occur in the bathroom, so taking some measures to protect them from harsh odors can be beneficial, too.

Creating an Accessible and Safe Bathroom

First and foremost, accessibility is going to be key for your child. So things like installing grab bars around the toilet and sink can really boost stability and independence. You might consider adding a raised toilet seat or a specialized toilet chair to make transferring easier if your child has difficulty moving independently. It's also important to ensure that the sink is at a reachable height, maybe with lever-style faucets that are easier to operate. A step stool with handrails can provide extra support for your child as they navigate getting onto the toilet or reaching the sink to wash their hands. As they're getting accustomed to the bathroom environment and using the toilet, it's always a good idea to supervise your child to keep them safe.

For kids with visual impairments specifically, you'll want to create a welcoming and accessible space that helps them navigate the bathroom safely. Using high-contrast colors can help distinguish different areas and items, such as the toilet, sink, and towel racks. Adding tactile markers or Braille labels on fixtures can empower your child to identify them by touch. Keeping pathways leading to the bathroom clear and using non-slip mats can prevent falls, and don't forget that verbal instructions and cues can guide your child through each step of the process as they become more familiar with the layout and routine, building their independence along the way.

Finally, it's super important to ensure that the bathroom is safe and child-proofed to prevent any accidents that might lead to fears or anxieties about the space. The last thing you want is for a fall or injury to validate your child's trepidations about potty training! Putting safety locks on cabinets, keeping cleaning supplies and medications out of reach, securely fastening all potty chairs or seat reducers, and using non-slip mats as needed will help prevent any mishaps. If you're able to create a safe and welcoming environment, it will make potty training a more positive experience for both you and your child!

Adding Adaptive Equipment to the Bathroom

Adaptive equipment plays a significant role in making the toilet easier to use for children with various disabilities. Sometimes adding equipment that modifies or aids in balance, posture, or physical support can make all the difference in the potty training process. Your occupational therapist may be able to make recommendations on the types of equipment that would be most beneficial for your child's specific needs. Some things to keep in mind when selecting your equipment include:

- Will the equipment help your child access the potty safely?
- Will the equipment help your child with their balance, supportive posture, or increased range of motion?
- Will the equipment address any unique sensory needs?
- Will the equipment provide added comfort and reassurance, making the toilet more inviting?

Here are some of the different types of adaptive equipment that can help with potty training:

Padded seat reducers. Several from Jool Baby® are linked in our product guide! Making the toilet as comfortable as possible can encourage and reassure your child. The soft padding provides a more secure feeling while sitting, which can be crucial for kids who have difficulty processing sensory information or physical disabilities that make it difficult or even painful to sit on hard surfaces. Your child may also be scared of the toilet's large opening, which is certainly understandable! The seat reducer will make the opening a more manageable size so they don't feel like they are at risk of being swallowed up. Choosing a seat reducer with padding, handles, or your child's favorite characters is a great way to make the toilet more comfortable and inviting.

Toilet seat inserts with ladder attachments. If your child has limited mobility, a toilet seat with a built-in ladder attachment (we love Jool Baby®'s Potty Training Seat with 2 Step Ladder!) can provide them with more support, balance, and stability, while still being able to get onto the toilet independently. If this sounds like a good option for your family, be sure you take into consideration your child's height as well as any sensory concerns. The step on the ladder should be high enough to allow their feet to rest on and

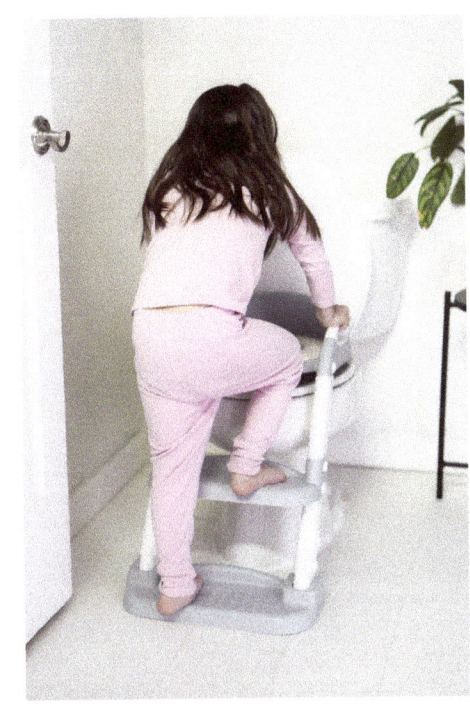

be flat and fully supported, so they are in an ideal physical posture for peeing and pooping. This also helps children to relax and focus on the task at hand as opposed to their legs dangling. Some of these inserts may also have higher handles or seat backs, splash guards, and/or padding for added comfort.

Bath–toilet systems. These types of toileting systems address physical needs at varying levels and provide consistent positioning to help with physical posture and support. For a child with severe motor impairment, using a toilet without one of these support systems may not be an option. It could be stationary and attach directly to the toilet as a more permanent fixture, which can allow your child to feel more empowered and confident while in the bathroom, or it also may be mobile, allowing it to be wheeled in and out of the shower or over the toilet. Some of these systems come with a commode attachment, which can make using the potty more convenient without actually being in the bathroom.

Grab bars/handles or arm rests. Adding handles or arm rests near or on the toilet can be helpful in many ways. Not only can this type of equipment help your child get onto and off of the toilet safely, but if your child struggles with balance or range of motion, they can use the handles to support and stabilize themselves while they are wiping or being wiped.

Step stools. You will hear me keep mentioning this - adequate foot support while using the toilet is super important during potty training and beyond, not just from a safety and accessibility standpoint, but for the actual acts of peeing and pooping as well. Good toileting posture, as noted above, aligns the rectum for easier and more complete elimination of the bowel without straining, reducing the risk of constipation and allowing for full voiding of the bladder as well. Step stools come in a variety of heights, so be sure to choose one that gives your child the support they need. Squatty Potty® has stools with options to alternate between different heights for growth and different family members. You can have your child sit on the toilet and measure the space between their feet and the floor, and then add a few inches to be sure it is tall enough to obtain that natural squat position. Keep in mind that as your child grows, the size of the step stool they need may change.

Standing support stations. These allow partially weight-bearing children to transfer to the toilet, have their clothing and diapers changed, or be wiped in an upright, standing position. As your child grows, this can reduce some of the heavy lifting to get them onto and off of the toilet, allows for pushing down and pulling up pants and underwear more easily, and helps you to wipe them more easily.

Faucet extenders. These handy gadgets assist kids during the potty training process by making hand washing more accessible and therefore encouraging good hygiene habits right from the start. Attached to the end of the faucet, a faucet extender brings the water flow further into the sink, which allows small children, or children who use wheelchairs, to easily access water without the need for step stools or adult assistance. This independence improves confidence and reinforces the importance of handwashing after using the toilet, promoting a routine of cleanliness that can be helpful in all aspects of your child's life!

Making the Bathroom Enjoyable

Turning the bathroom into a comfortable, enjoyable, and inviting environment can bring a ton of positivity to your potty training experience. You can start by simply making the space visually appealing through your child's eyes. Decorate the bathroom with bright, cheerful colors and fun, child-friendly themes. Wall decals featuring favorite characters or animals can create an engaging atmosphere. Personalizing the bathroom with your child's favorite things can make it feel more like their own special space.

One of my favorite things to do is head to the dollar store and pick up some themed décor—it can be for an upcoming holiday, a particular interest your child has, or a random mix of things! Your child will actually want to be in the bathroom if the space is made appealing with some cool new stuff to look at while they're sitting on the potty. You can also make a little potty caddy with some fun and new activities your child can do during potty time. Fidget or sensory toys, bubbles, sticker books, or even old household items that they might not normally get to play with are all great options to include. Let yourself get creative and have fun with it, too!

Also be sure to incorporate child-sized equipment to increase comfort and accessibility whenever possible. A small potty chair near the toilet or a padded toilet seat insert as discussed earlier in this chapter can make the experience less intimidating and more manageable. Adding a step stool with non-slip features can help your child reach the toilet and the sink independently, helping to create a sense of autonomy.

If your child struggles with being in the bathroom or sitting on the toilet, you can incorporate some fun, interactive elements to make their bathroom experience actually feel enjoyable! Waterproof books, bath toys, or stickers can keep your child entertained, relaxed, and even distracted during potty sessions. A reward chart with stickers or magnets can add motivation by visually tracking their progress and celebrating their successes. Dimming the lights, playing soft, calming music, adding an oil diffuser, or burning a candle can also help create a soothing environment that reduces anxiety and makes the bathroom an inviting place. Other ideas might be a lava or bubble lamp, an artificial fish tank, or a seek-and-find poster to put at eye level across from the potty, if possible.

By creating a supportive environment tailored to their needs, your child is more likely to develop positive associations with the bathroom and using the potty!

Amanda and Colbie: Physical Accessibility Concerns in Public Restrooms

We started potty training when Colbie was around two-and-a-half years old. It was right in the middle of the world shutting down for COVID-19 and we had a baby on the way, so I figured there was no better time to get her out of diapers. From an actual training perspective, potty training was fairly easy for us. Being a special education teacher, I took a very reinforcement-heavy approach. I would sit her on a kid potty every 15 minutes and she got one M&M for sitting and two for going. Once she was dry for two days like that, I expanded the time by 15-minute intervals, and she caught on pretty quickly!

The biggest issue we had and still do with toileting is making it an accessible and independent experience. Colbie has cerebral palsy and she is older now than she was when we trained several years ago, so she wants her independence as well her privacy in the bathroom. Being that she does not have balance mastered, finding a potty seat that lets her get up on to the real toilet has been hard. At home, she is able to climb up with a step, but these seats don't usually come with handles tall enough for the child to stand and then pull their pants up using them. We trialed many and finally found one that has higher handles, but still, the balance required to then pull her pants back up before stepping down has been a real challenge as well as a safety concern.

In public restrooms, our choices are that she starts independently in the regular stall and I cram myself in to help her if she ends up needing me, or she loses out on the learning and privacy by having me help the entire time in an accessible stall—it's not ideal either way.

When out in public, the thing I have noticed is that there are accessible bathrooms, but the toilets in those stalls are extra high. This is a bad combination for children with disabilities who need the grab bar but can't get up to the tall toilet. Colbie has actually been going into the normal stall on her own because the walls are closer and she can use them in lieu of a bar. But she will also need to hold the toilet seat as she's shimmying herself on, which nobody wants to touch if they don't have to! And then when she's done, she needs to be able to reach the toilet paper, which requires maneuvering with balance. We still have issues now with wiping after a bowel movement due to range of motion and continue to work on that.

Adaptive clothing has been an amazing addition to Colbie's wardrobe, not just for dressing but for toileting. She can pull down her pants on her own, but with differing strength between her left and right hands, she utilizes the loops sewn into adaptive pants to get them back up evenly. This solves some of our issues with pants, though Colbie loves wearing dresses and wanted to wear a dress to school just like her friends do. However, we avoided them for a while because it was an added challenge in the bathroom. Knowing this, her 1:1 at school came up with a system where she'll use a hair elastic to tie her dress up (she wears leggings underneath) before entering the bathroom, so this way Colbie gets to wear a dress if she chooses and doesn't lose her privacy as a result. It was so nice that someone besides me came up with a simple adaptation so that she could express her identity as she wanted to!

Colbie is always working so hard on her balance and mobility, and these challenges evolve through the years just as she does. I'm not sure I realized when we originally potty trained that the actual training was going to be the easy part, but we're always finding new ways to adapt as we discover new tools and develop new skills. My wish is that companies would keep coming up with child-friendly devices and aids for both training and public bathrooms!

Chapter 8: Visual Learning

Using visual aids during potty training can be a game changer, especially when your child has a disability. Visual learning is so powerful because it taps into the natural way many children process information. Studies have shown that children, in general, are more likely to learn better visually, with about 65% of the population being classified as visual learners.[8] This is because visual information is processed faster and retained longer than auditory information.

Visual learning tools are also extremely helpful if your child has been diagnosed with speech and language delays because it can give them a way to understand new processes and communicate needs and choices. Of course traditional potty training books and videos are great, but there are other types of visual aids to explore as well. If your child is non- or preverbal, struggles with communication, and/or has a cognitive delay, you may consider getting some printable potty charts or task schedules that show each step of potty use. Additionally, social stories are commonly used with children who have autism and similar learning profiles to help explain new concepts. Flash cards can also be helpful to add to your toolkit. Let's go over some of the most common types of visual aids and explore the benefits of each.

Potty Books

One of my absolute favorite ways to introduce new concepts to kids, potty training of course included, is through books. There are so many great options out there when it comes to potty training books for kids, and you don't have to wait until you're ready to start the actual potty training process to read them! Reading books about using the potty is a great way to introduce the concept and get them familiar with it in a low-pressure, stress-free way. When choosing a potty book, look for engaging illustrations that show all different aspects of potty use. You can get a variety of books—simple picture books that are more step-by-step and instructional, books that are silly and funny, or books that have interactive features like flaps to lift or buttons to press that make sounds. Think about your child's unique preferences and what they would enjoy. Each day, try to incorporate at least one potty book—and you can rotate them to keep things fresh—so it starts to plant the seed in a seamless way.

Potty Videos

Similar to potty books, potty videos are a great way to help your child learn about potty training. You can find tons of different potty videos and apps online. If your child has a certain amount of screen time each day, make one of the videos they watch about the potty. This helps pique your child's interests about the potty, but they don't necessarily realize they're learning because they're just watching a video. It's a win-win! One note is to preview the video first, as you would with any online content.

Social Stories

A social story is a visual tool that helps children understand certain situations in a very literal way. Developed by Carol Gray in the early 1990s, social stories were initially designed to help individuals with autism understand social interactions and expectations. These stories are designed to be easily understood, with clear, concise language and supportive illustrations or photographs.

Social stories are particularly beneficial for children with ASD, because they often struggle with social cues and transitions or changes in their routine. However, they are also useful for children with other developmental disabilities or even typically developing children who benefit from clear, structured guidance. In the context of potty training, a social story might explain the steps involved, such as recognizing the need to go, getting to the bathroom, using the toilet or potty, wiping, flushing, and washing hands. With both a visual and narrative framework, your child can better understand the process, which provides them with predictability to reduce stress or anxiety.

The beauty of a social story is that you can actually create your own custom story at home for free! Making your own social story about potty training for your child can be a fun way to get them familiar with the process. You can start by taking photographs of your child in different stages of the potty training routine. For example, take a photo of your child in a pose that might say, "I need the potty!"; of them in front of the toilet pushing down their pants; of them sitting on the toilet, then wiping, flushing, and washing their hands. You can also include pictures of your family and caregivers offering encouragement or help, making it a supportive and positive experience. Having photographs of the bathrooms in your home or the potty your child will be using can make the story more realistic. Just arrange your photos in order and write simple, clear captions to go with each picture. Use language that your child understands, like, "When I need to go potty, I tell my grown up," and, "I push down my pants and underwear and sit on the toilet." Make it as specific to your child's situation as possible to not only help them learn all the steps of potty training, but also for added confidence and consistency.

Visual Task Schedules

Visual task schedules, also known as visual schedules or task schedules, are another excellent tool for potty training. These are printed sequences of images or symbols that outline each step of a task or routine. For example, a visual task schedule for potty training might include photos or graphics of a toilet, pants down, a child sitting on the toilet, a wipe or toilet paper, a hand flushing the toilet, and washing hands. You might wish to print out and laminate a potty training task schedule to hang up in your bathroom while your child is learning. When you're working on modeling potty use, especially if you have a child who is not yet verbal, they can point to the step in the process that comes next.

You can create a custom one that even looks like your child from our friends at Focus Posters (linked in our product guide in Chapter 6), or you can make your own.

These schedules are beneficial because they provide a clear, predictable, step-by-step structure that children can easily follow, making abstract concepts more understandable. They are particularly helpful for children with ADHD, ASD, and other developmental delays, as

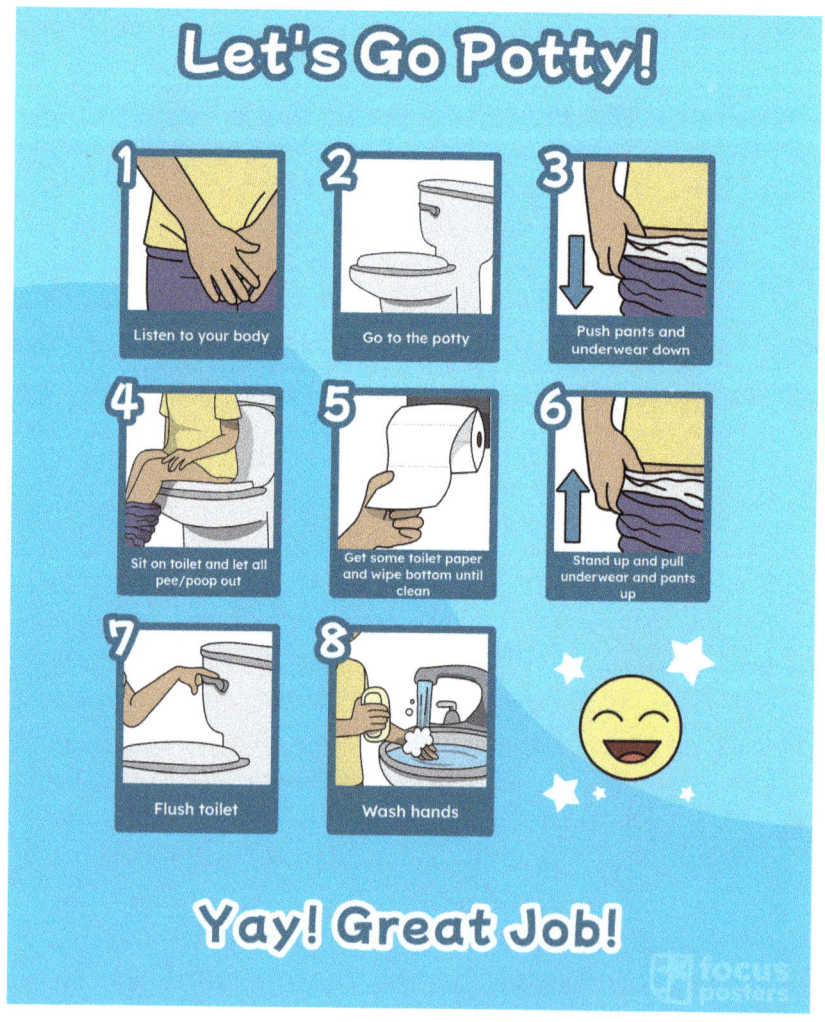

well as for those who simply thrive on routine and visual instruction. By breaking down the potty training process into manageable steps, visual task schedules can help your child gain their potty independence.

Flash Cards

Flash cards are generally small cards that contain a picture or word on one side and a corresponding description or explanation on the other. They are commonly used to teach vocabulary and concepts, and in the case of potty training, they can be very helpful. Flash cards can depict various aspects of the potty training process, such as a toilet, toilet paper, soap, and different emotions related to using the bathroom.

Flash cards can help your child learn the vocabulary associated with potty training and can also be used to reinforce steps and routines. Having a flash card for the potty versus the regular toilet, or poop versus pee, or two different options in rewards can help your child communicate their choices to you about their potty use, and any way you can offer choices is a great way to encourage independence and cooperation!

Each type of visual aid brings its own special benefit to potty training. They are not only helpful during the prep phase, but can and should be carried over into the training phase as well. Don't discount this super simple strategy to help your child get excited about the process. They'll be learning without even realizing it!

Chapter 9: One Step at a Time

Creating a potty routine for your child can make the potty training process less stressful for both of you. Establishing a consistent potty schedule helps your child understand what to expect throughout their daily routine, which is especially beneficial for children who thrive on predictability. Let's discuss how to come up with a potty schedule that makes sense for your child so that they can not only use the potty successfully, but start to learn how to recognize their body's natural urges to pee and poop.

Knowing When and How Often to Go

When you first start potty training, you might be tempted to set a timer and take your child to sit on the potty every 20 or 30 minutes. You may even just have them set up camp on the potty and encourage them to sit *until* they go. You might find yourself constantly asking, "Do you need to go potty? What about now? It's been a few minutes, do you need to go yet? I think we should try again!" Actually these are all great ways to get pee or poop into the potty, making it seem like a surefire way to achieve success. But ultimately, the end goal of potty training isn't to solely prevent accidents, it's to encourage your child to learn how to listen to their body and either notify someone or take themselves to the potty when they feel that natural urge. By using these methods, you run the risk of your child never learning the signals their body sends them about when to go potty because you've already prompted them to go. Not to mention, you can unintentionally create frustration, resistance, and big power struggles by prompting your child to sit on the potty too often or for too long.

To pass urine easily, the bladder muscle needs to contract while the pelvic floor muscles relax. That doesn't happen as easily or naturally if there's no signal or urge within the body to go. Your child might be able to squeeze out a little bit of pee, but that's only because the bladder is contracting more aggressively to make it happen. Additionally, if the bladder is always being emptied before it has reached its full capacity, it will start to "think" it's full when it's actually not. Then your child could just end up feeling like they have to pee a lot more frequently, and when they do go, it's not how their body is naturally designed to work.

As I've been saying throughout the book, every child is unique when it comes to potty training and their bladder capacity and urge frequency is no different. Some children need to pee every few minutes. But also, some children only need to pee every few hours. Both fall in the range of being perfectly normal. And when you first start potty training, you won't necessarily know where in that range your child falls in order to schedule potty visits into their routine. This is where you'll be learning about your child's potty habits in the first few days without diapers. Try to jot down some notes about how often your child seems to need to go, or if there are certain times of day that they are more likely to go. This might result in more accidents initially, but it allows you to look out for any physical cues or signals so you can try to help them learn those signs for themselves, while also setting them up for successful visits to the potty.

Potty Language

Most children give some sort of physical sign or cue when they feel the urge to go, but at first they might not recognize what their body is telling them. Your child is used to wearing diapers, so they've never needed to pay much attention to those signals before, and certain factors associated with disabilities may make this part of the process more challenging. This is another thing that you will be learning in the first few days without diapers, or as you give your child practice without diapers leading up to formal potty training. The signals, or "potty language" as I like to call it, can include a wide variety of changes in behavior or emotions, from super obvious to very subtle. Since you're the expert on your child, you'll likely pick up on this fairly quickly.

Some examples of how a child might physically display their need to use the potty would be:

- Crossing their legs
- Grabbing or playing with their genitals or their bottom
- Walking around on tiptoes
- Not being able to stand still—a.k.a.,doing the potty dance

Behaviorally, their energy level might seem to spike, they could get clingy or irritable, or they might try to run off and hide. When needing to poop, some children freeze and stand completely still, stare off into space, get angry or aggressive when approached, or suddenly get red in the face from straining. If you start noticing any of these signs from your child, you know it's a good time to prompt a visit to the potty. To take this learning one step further so they can eventually self-initiate, help them recognize that their body is sending them these signs which means it's potty time! Say, "I can see you are crossing your legs. That's your body's way of telling you it needs to go potty. Come on, let's go sit!" If your child is non- or preverbal, this is a great place to use a flash card or teach your child the sign language for this vocabulary.

Keep in mind that children with disabilities may have symptoms or characteristics that inhibit their ability to sense a natural urge to use the bathroom. This means that it could take longer for them to learn how to self-initiate. In fact, some children may never gain this ability, which leaves them to rely on a set potty schedule.

Potty Breaks at Transitional Times

After learning a bit about your child's natural elimination habits— meaning how often they need to go, or if there are certain times of day that they tend to need to go—you can create a potty schedule that fits into your child's existing daily routine. Schedule potty breaks during transitional times, such as first thing in the morning, after meals, and before bed. These are natural breaks in the day as you move from one activity to the next. Making a potty visit part of these transitions as opposed to stopping another activity in order to go to the bathroom helps reinforce the new routine of using the potty and this predictability can reduce anxiety, prevent resistance, and make it easier for your child to anticipate when it's time to use the potty. It also ensures that they have enough opportunities to practice and get comfortable with using the potty, which is especially helpful as you first get started. Over time, your child's potty needs may change, so their frequency or timing can shift accordingly.

In addition to using the potty at home at set times each day, you can have your child try to use the potty before leaving the house or before starting a stimulating activity, such as attending a music class or birthday party, for example, until they are in a solid routine of using the potty reliably on their own.

Using a Visual Schedule

As I mentioned in Chapter 8, a visual schedule can be a powerful tool in potty training. Creating a chart that shows the times your child will use the potty throughout their day can make the routine more predictable and easier to understand. Visual schedules provide clear cues and reminders, helping your child anticipate what activity comes next. You can use pictures or symbols to represent different activities, such as getting dressed, brushing teeth, and eating breakfast, as well as potty times, making it easier for children who

have difficulty with verbal instructions. This visual aid can reduce anxiety and power struggles as well as increase your child's confidence in managing their day. Our friends at Focus Posters even let you create custom visual schedules that look like your child!

Bottomless Time

Providing your child some bottomless or naked time during potty training can really accelerate their learning, and here's why: First, it helps them become more aware of what's happening with their body. Until now, they've had a diaper to absorb any moisture or contain poop, which means they likely never paid much attention to when they were actually releasing. But when they're bottomless, the pee and poop come with no barrier, which creates a little "aha!" moment. They'll gradually realize that there's no diaper to contain things, encouraging them to take action. This time also helps them start connecting the feelings and urges in their body to the need to get to the potty before it's too late, or at least to notify you that something's coming.

Second, this strategy helps you as well. During diaper-free days, you'll begin learning your child's natural potty habits and routines, giving you the chance to catch them in the act and get them to the potty. Eventually you may be able to develop a predictable voiding schedule to help potty use fit into your daily routine around the times your child is likely to naturally need to go. It's much easier to notice these things when they're bottomless than when they're wearing underwear or a diaper, where elimination might go unnoticed until the learning opportunity has passed. I know this might feel overwhelming at first, but trust me, the initial mess and hard work will pay off in the end!

Moving from Diapers to Underwear

For some families, gradually transitioning from diapers to underwear makes the most sense. Potty training without a deadline allows your child to get used to the feel and function of underwear at their own pace, which naturally reduces pressure and stress for everyone involved. Disposable pull-on training underwear can be a helpful learning tool if this seems like the right fit for your family. These training pants are designed with an elastic waistband instead of fastening at the sides like a diaper, making them easy to pull up and down so that they resemble underwear. This can build your child's confidence in managing their clothing while providing protection for accidents, which can be a good way to bridge the gap between diapers and underwear. Starting with disposable training underwear during the day while still using diapers at night can ease the transition to using the potty full time. You can choose to practice time in underwear or sitting on the potty at certain times when it is convenient for the family, allowing your child to get some exposure to the potty or toilet before saying goodbye to diapers for good. As your child becomes more comfortable and confident with using the potty, you can gradually switch to regular underwear.

Pro-tip from Taryn: *Find a disposable training pant that has hook-and-loop sides rather than ones that only rip to come off. The latter requires clothing, shoes and, if you have them, orthotics to be removed in order to change into a clean one.*

When following this type of approach, remember to maintain realistic expectations and give yourself, and your child, plenty of grace. Since you won't have strict expectations on potty use, it could make the process take several months or more before your child is ready to switch to regular underwear. In fact, some families might never feel fully confident in removing disposable training pants or diapers completely, and if you and your child are satisfied with that reality, then that is perfectly okay!

On the other hand, some families might find it more effective to make a firm switch from diapers to underwear over the course of a few days. This generally provides clear expectations to your child that a new phase has begun and can oftentimes accelerate the potty training process. Moving directly from diapers to underwear instead of using disposable training underwear leaves no room for confusion and sends a clear, consistent message that all pee and poop belongs in the potty from now on. In many cases, it is completely possible to lay the foundation for potty use within just a few days' time. This approach requires dedication and commitment from you and your child's caregivers to ensure that the new expectations can be followed consistently, allowing progress to advance. That doesn't mean that there won't be messy days mixed in with the successful days, especially at first, but by eliminating diapers from the start, it will send a clear message to your child with no ambiguity.

In most cases for children with disabilities, it makes sense to focus on daytime potty training before removing nighttime diapers. Nighttime dryness isn't something that can always be easily controlled, especially for children whose disability might impact their muscle tone, interoception, motor coordination, communication skills, or mobility. Helping your child get into a good routine with their daytime potty use will allow them to gain confidence in learning the steps of using the potty, as well as give them practice with listening and responding to their body's natural urges.

Once these skill sets are well established, you can decide if your child is ready to sleep through the night without diapers. Occasionally, as daytime bladder control improves, it will carry over into nighttime as well and your child could start waking up with dry diapers on their own. At this point, your child is likely physically capable, so you can make the switch over to sleeping in underwear. I'll have more tips on helping your child achieve nighttime dryness in Chapter 12.

Whether you choose a gradual transition or a more immediate switch, the goal is to make the process as smooth and stress-free as possible. Celebrate every step forward, and remember that progress may be slow and steady, especially at first. Again, every child is different, and the best approach depends on their unique needs and readiness. The key is to be flexible and responsive to your child's progress, making adjustments as needed to support their success.

Here are some examples of things you can say to your child while they are sitting on the potty to encourage success. Keep in mind that many children who have a disability also have a natural affinity to music. Turning any of these statements into a song for added engagement can help reduce anxiety and promote learning!

"Just relax and let the pee flow out."

"Let's take some deep breaths to help the poop come out."

*"You are doing the right thing.
Pee/poop wants to be in the potty!"*

*"Your body will feel so much better after you
let the pee/poop out!"*

"Pee and poop belong in the potty! You can do this!"

"Listen carefully. What does your pee sound like?"

Undressing and Dressing

Helping your child learn to dress and undress themselves during potty training is an exciting step toward building independence. Of course, different disabilities come with their own set of associated challenges when it comes to dressing. For example, a child with fine motor delays might find buttons or zippers tricky, while a child with limited mobility or a limb difference might struggle to grip and pull up their pants. Children with cognitive disabilities may need extra time and repetition to understand the steps involved.

Just remember, this is a skill that can be developed gradually as other potty training steps are being mastered. It's okay if this part feels challenging—keeping your expectations realistic is key. It's completely normal for your child to need some help with dressing and undressing, and if they're not quite ready for this yet, that's perfectly fine. It shouldn't stop you from moving forward with other parts of potty training. This is a journey, and each child progresses at their own pace. Be patient with both yourself and your child as you work through these skills together.

To empower your child, start by choosing clothing that's easy to manage, like pants with elastic waistbands, avoiding buttons or zippers. You can even choose to go up a size so the clothing has a looser fit and therefore is easier to grip and pull. Having loose, lightweight fabrics, and limiting clothing layers will also help with urge recognition and accident awareness, which will accelerate their learning. In some cases, it can help a child learn more quickly by wearing only loose-fitting shorts or pants, or a dress with nothing underneath at first so they have less clothing to manipulate and fewer layers to minimize sensations. This will also feel less like the diapers that they have been used to wearing, acting as a continual subliminal message to not void their bladder or bowels. So many types of adaptive clothing can make the process more manageable, while promoting independence and inclusion as well.

Break down the steps of going to the bathroom into small, manageable tasks, and provide clear, simple instructions, being mindful of the language that you use. For example, instead of saying "Pull down your pants," which, when taken literally, can be a bit confusing, you can say, "Push down your pants." Be sure you are framing the instructions in ways that make sense for your child's cognitive level. If you are working with an occupational therapist or speech language pathologist, they may be able to give you some specific tips based on your child's unique abilities. Work on these skills outside of potty time, which will allow your child to practice and learn without the added pressure of actually needing to use the bathroom. It can be a big confidence blow if your child has an accident simply because they aren't able to get their pants down in time. Staging fashion shows or dress-up sessions are fun ways to refine this skill!

As with all steps of potty training, it's important to be patient and celebrate small victories. Some children may always need assistance with dressing and undressing, depending on their disability. Ultimately, the goal is to promote as much independence as possible while providing the necessary support to help your child feel successful.

Kristi & Theo:
Commitment, Consistency, and Clorox Wipes

Apparently, I was potty trained by the time I was 16 months old. It's one of my mom's favorite fun facts to share when talking about her kids' milestones. I have always accepted it as truth and never raised an eyebrow, but two kids later, I've got some serious suspicions.

Of course, being identified as an overachiever in this department myself, I had high hopes for my kids. When my son Theo was nearing his second birthday, I was confident it was time to give it a try. But Theo? He had zero interest. And, in true boy fashion, he didn't even bother to protest. He just gave the toilet, and me, a blank stare, like it was some pointless obstacle standing between him and his next movie or favorite toy. We would try again a few times between age two and age four with little success. However, as parents, we were still missing vital pieces of information about who Theo was and how his brain worked. On his third birthday, Theo was diagnosed with autism, and my understanding of what that could mean for his adaptive skills—toileting included—wouldn't come until much later.

When Theo started his first school program that fall, I brought up potty training with his teacher. Her response is forever burned into my brain: "Potty training before age four is a social construct." Ms. Brittney might not realize it, but her words—and people like her—became my gold standard for deciding who truly has my kid's best interest at heart.

Any special needs parent knows the endless comparisons to "typical" peers. We're bombarded with lists, scores, and assessments that inject fear into our parenting journey. So, when someone like Ms. Brittney comes along and offers much-needed reassurance that some things aren't worth stressing over right now, it's a breath of fresh air. It gives us permission to see our kids as individuals and value their developmental trajectory versus viewing everything through the lens of a diagnosis.

Thanks to Ms. Brittney, we hit pause on our potty training attempts and spent a year helping Theo get comfortable in his new program. As he entered his second year of preschool, his lovely teacher, Ms. G., decided it was time to try again.

I'm not a huge fan of bribery. I just don't love the energy it brings to parenting, plus Theo has never been motivated by it. Potty training felt like a valid exception, and Ms. G. told us food would be the ideal reinforcer, so we brought it in. I can't remember how long it took him to learn, but I do remember the food reinforcers being sent back home untouched. At home, we really upped the ante—I'm pretty sure I spent a solid $250.00 on Pixar Cars. The cars worked, but I still don't know what drove the initial success at school. To this day, I feel as though both myself and my bank account may have been played.

Naturally, the second Theo started to see success at school, he seemed to figure out how his body worked and stopped drinking during the day. I guess he wanted to limit how often he had to practice. Being his mom, I knew there was one thing that would get him sipping first thing in the AM, but I refused to send him in with a soda, so I started sending him with a Starbucks iced tea instead. Theo has always done bougie well, and the Starbucks worked. For anyone keeping score: Theo = 2, Mommy's bank account = 0.

Looking back, "number one" was easy. "Number two," well, that took some serious creativity. Theo is very visual, but he's also very literal, so any visuals have to match the activity almost exactly to make sense. Maybe I'm a terrible parent, but I did not have the stomach to go into google and come out with an adequate set of visuals to sell him on the idea of going number two in the potty. So, instead, we opted for theatrics and spent a lot of time watching the "Cocomelon poop video" while on the toilet. We sang, we laughed, we said "eeeew it smells…," and we grunted until he made it happen one day when I was solo-parenting. I was so excited, I think I texted all my friends. In short, Mom finally scored a point, though in the end it was Theo's, also.

Demand avoidance excluded, Theo is still a routine-driven kid and his initial potty routine included stripping down, completely, for anything that involved the bathroom. He eventually found his way to redressing before leaving the bathroom, and then kindergarten happened.

I learned the hard way that not all special needs programs are created equal. Combine "errorless learning" with Theo's well disguised perfectionism, and what do you get? Regression. The result? My almost fully potty-trained kiddo suddenly started leaving the bathroom with his pants down and looking for an adult to help.

Although potty training wasn't why we switched programs, it was a prime example of why we needed to. We spent the summer after kindergarten dedicated to moving, exploring, and a therapy called DIR/Floortime. When the DIR supervisor first came over for an assessment, Theo did his usual thing and went to the potty independently and came out with his pants down. It was on a list of things I thought we needed to "tackle head on…" and our supervisor looked at him and said, "Oh, that's it? I wouldn't worry about that, he will figure that out…" So, we stopped worrying and we stayed consistent.

For those unfamiliar, DIR/Floortime is a developmentally-based therapy that focuses on natural growth stages rather than rigid behavioral interventions. Outside of sessions, it taught us to create a safe environment for Theo, to breathe deeply, and to prioritize family relationships over meeting demands. It fundamentally changed the way we view autism in our home and gave us the confidence to build a world for Theo centered on both psychological safety and the nurturing of his development.

[9]Our most recent set of potty-training victories have come three years after that initial success. Theo learned, through modeling, that you actually need to remove the toilet paper from the roll before using it (yes, there are stories here that I won't share, haha). And, in a triumphant twist, he randomly decided it was time to stand up while peeing—no more stripping down. His confidence has skyrocketed, proven by his somewhat stoic and bold stance when he decides to leverage his new skills to pee outside, which hilariously enough is another big win. We are big outdoors people, and it is no fun leaving a hike or a nature class simply because the woods or a porta-potty won't cut it.

My advice for potty training isn't much different from my advice for all things autism and special needs parenting: take a deep breath. Meet your kid where they are, and don't let fear drive the ship—easier said than done, but it's worth it. Approach every challenge with curiosity and compassion, and never fail to give yourself grace. Remember that time is in fact your friend, not your enemy. Celebrate hard, no matter how big or small the achievement. And if you're potty training a boy? Keep a screwdriver and your favorite disinfectant nearby because you'll definitely need to take the toilet apart to clean up all the extra pee while he works on his aim.

Chapter 10: Handling Successes, Accidents, and Resistance

The entire process of potty training can seem like a roller coaster ride. You'll be riding high one day, but feeling stuck the next. Rest assured that this is perfectly normal, and more often than not, you'll be back on top soon enough!

Let's explore some practical, effective strategies for handling your child's potty training successes, accidents, and any resistance you might encounter in between.

Handling Successes

First, take a minute to define success for your child. Whether that be your child starting to have an accident, but then getting some pee or poop into the potty either from your redirection or them realizing and going themselves, your child agreeably using the potty when prompted by you, or them self-initiating and going to sit on the potty all on their own; these are all great examples of potty training successes. But remember, at first, it's not all about pee or poop making it into the potty. If your child really struggles with transitions, which is a common trait for many types of disabilities, success might just be your child agreeing to be in the bathroom near the toilet. Find any of those small wins and celebrate accordingly! Positive reinforcement with verbal and physical praise, and even rewards or incentives, can be super motivating for kids adjusting to this new diaper-free phase.

For any type of success, you're most likely going to start off with general verbal praise. It helps to be specific, and say things to try and trigger their intrinsic, or internal, motivation. For example, "Great job putting your pee in the potty! You should be so proud!" Combine that with some physical affection—a hug, a fist bump, or a high five—and you're really in business! Most kids love being acknowledged by their parents or caregivers for an accomplishment, so this can be extremely inspiring for them to use the potty again and again.

That said, of course you'll want to be careful to consider how your child responds to loud sounds or sudden movements. Sometimes, your squeal of excitement over them using the potty can unintentionally startle them and drive your progress backwards. Some children don't like attention drawn to themselves, so if that applies to your situation, it's perfectly okay to be more nonchalant about their success.

Here are some scripts that you can use after your child has successfully used the potty. Also remember to be specific and pair these with physical praise, too, if that is something your child enjoys.

"You peed/pooped in the potty! Way to go!"

"You should be so proud of yourself for putting your pee in the potty!"

"Great job listening to your body and putting your poop in the potty!"

"I bet your belly feels so much better now that you put your pee in the potty!"

"You did it! You put your pee in the potty! Wasn't that fast? Now you can get right back to playing!"

Using Rewards

Providing rewards can be a pretty controversial topic with a lot of conflicting opinions. Ultimately, you'll have to decide what aligns with your family's values, but if you're on the fence, research shows that using rewards has more advantages than disadvantages. According to an article written by parenting expert, Alan Kazdin, in 2021,[10] rewards help children to get "repeated practice" of a non-preferred activity, i.e., an activity they don't love doing (such as toileting), which then turns into a habit.

Some might argue that rewards can decrease a child's intrinsic motivation to successfully use the toilet. But an article by Cameron, Banko, and Pierce in 2001[11] that combines decades of research finds that rewards do not decrease intrinsic motivation. According to this review, rewards only decrease internal motivation if:

- The activity is already of high interest to your child, which is unlikely to be true at this stage of potty training.
- The reward is automatically expected or is promised beforehand, more like a bribe.
- The reward is not clearly related to performance, meaning the reward isn't given immediately or consistently after successfully using the toilet.

In addition, parenting training programs that use rewards have been found to have significant and long-lasting improvements in child behavior, as found by Long, Forehand, Wierson, and Morgan in 1994.[12] And the use of rewards can actually improve the parent-child relationship, as found by Wiggins, Sofronoff, and Sanders in 2009.[13]

When it comes to choosing a reward or reinforcer for your child, you're going to want to select something that is really desirable to them. I'm not saying that you have to go out and buy them a new bike every time they use the potty, of course, but it is helpful if it isn't something they get access to on a regular basis. The reward can be something edible (like a cookie or popsicle), something tangible (like a new toy car or small party favor), or something experiential (like watching a show or painting their fingernails). A little bonus tip: you can make the reward even more enticing by adding in an element of surprise. Wrapping each prize and keeping them all in a small basket, making a surprise box that they can reach into, or using an advent calendar where they can randomly open a door to find a new prize are all ways to add in more fun!

Whichever reward you decide to go with, keep it exclusive to potty successes. Depending on what you have defined as success for your child or where you are in the learning process, this might look like just sitting on the potty, or you might reserve the reward for pee or poop making it into the potty. Keep in mind that even if it starts off as an accident but your child is then able to get some pee or poop into the potty, then that would count as a success and can be rewarded as such. As the research highlights above, you're going to want to give them the reward consistently and immediately after they've finished using the potty to help make the connection between the behavior and the prize. If you are using a visual schedule for potty training, be sure to have their reward listed as the final step in the process so your child knows what to expect.

Once your child has been using the potty reliably for a week or two, the habit is likely ingrained enough to where you can start cutting back on offering a reward for every success. Just be wary of stopping the rewards cold turkey, unless your child has already lost interest in them. Instead, wean off of the rewards gradually. You can start by setting slightly longer-term goals that can be kept track of on a chart or calendar instead of rewarding each individual potty success. Each time you increase the goal, increase the value of the reward to match. So instead of a single mini marshmallow for each pee in the potty, make s'mores after dinner for a great potty day. For a successful potty week, you can take them shopping and let them choose their own toy from the store. Eventually, your child will be able and willing to use the potty all on their own without receiving something in return.

In addition to a special potty reward, I would recommend pairing it with a very simple sticker chart as well. And when I say simple, I mean simple. This can literally be just a white piece of printer paper that they get to place a sticker on for each potty attempt or success. As simple as it is, this paper becomes a great visual representation of all the times they used the potty throughout the day, and it's a super fun thing to celebrate together as a family at the end of each day during the early phases of learning.

Handling Accidents

Along with starting to get some successes, there will more likely than not be a fair share of accidents to go along with them, especially during the first few diaper-free days. And trust me, I know as a busy parent myself that you are balancing multiple responsibilities along with potty training. When you first say goodbye to diapers, and even throughout the learning process, you won't be able to catch all the pee and poop in the potty; accidents are bound to happen. Dealing with accidents is without question one of the most daunting and frustrating parts of potty training. But accidents are a completely normal part of the process, and believe it or not, are actually a crucial part of your child's learning and mastery of the potty.

Think about it like this: Everyone makes mistakes when first learning a new skill, it's only natural. But science shows that every time we make a mistake, our brain works overtime to generate new pathways to prevent us from making that same mistake again in the future. Try to remind yourself of that as you're down in the trenches. It's important to try to be patient and calm and not get too frustrated. Many people tend to keep track of the number of accidents during potty training as a way to gauge progress, but really you should only be keeping track of the successes. That said, no one expects you to be perfect! It's okay if you do end up getting frustrated, but try your best to focus on all the good stuff you're seeing instead.

In the very beginning, accidents are simply due to the fact that your child doesn't yet possess the muscle control or awareness to make it to the potty in time. They are used to being able to just let go whenever, wherever, because their diapers have always been there to save the day. Forgetting that muscle memory of automatic release can take some time to unlearn. If your child's disability includes hypotonia or delayed interoception as a characteristic, it might take even more time for them to fully gain control.

But even once your child's muscle control and urge recognition improves and they start to really understand the concept of using the potty, accidents can still occur, and this is normal. Many times, accidents come as a result of your child being distracted. If they are engrossed in an activity, like playing outside, for example, two things tend to occur: Number one, they are less aware of the sensation of needing to go potty until it starts happening, and number two, they will hold it in so they don't have to stop the activity, potentially until it's too late. This is especially true for children who have ADHD, sensory processing disorders, or underdeveloped interoception. Accidents are also more likely to occur when your child is sick, very tired, or excited.

Whatever the reason for the accident, there should never be any shaming, scolding, or punishment. Remember, accidents are a natural part of learning this new skill. At the same time, you don't necessarily want to be too comforting either, because that could actually make your child falsely believe that accidents are acceptable. A minimal, matter-of-fact reaction works best. If you aren't able to catch any pee or poop in the potty once the accident starts, simply acknowledge the situation by stating what happened, and remind them of the new expectation.

Here are some examples of things you might say after your child has an accident without making it to the potty:

"Oops, you peed on the floor. Remember, pee only goes in the potty now. You can try again next time."

"Next time you get that feeling in your tummy, just let me know and I'll help you get to the potty."

"Poop goes in the potty! Come on, let's pick this up and put it in the potty where it belongs."

"Oops, you peed in your underwear. It's uncomfortable to wear wet clothes! We have to stop playing and get you cleaned up."

If your child is upset by an accident:

"We all make mistakes when we learn new things!
You'll be able to try again next time!"

"The important thing is that the pee and poop came out of
your body when it was ready. Next time we can put it in the
potty. I know you can do it!"

After an accident, you can take your child to the bathroom to clean
them up and change their clothes. However, avoid sitting them on the
potty or toilet after an accident has occurred. If they already had an accident, they probably don't have any pee or poop left to put in the toilet.

Children with intellectual or neurodevelopmental disabilities might
easily confuse the sequence of events, thinking that first they pee or
poop and then they sit on the potty. We only want to associate the
potty or toilet with the act of peeing or pooping so your child understands the true purpose and expectation.

Persistent Accidents

If you find that accidents are persistent and not improving, it can help
to exaggerate the cleanup process. You don't want your child thinking
that having an accident is more convenient than using the potty. Be
sure they stop playing until everything is cleaned up, and do a thor-
ough wipe-down or even bathe them before changing their clothes.
This shows your child that it is faster to just use the potty initially
instead of going in their pants or on the floor. You can also have them
participate in the cleanup if you think that would be a deterrent based
on your child's personality. If you decide to use this tactic, remember it should not be as a form of punishment, rather as an automatic
and consistent result to the behavior. To further drive this home, when
your child does use the potty, you can comment on how fast it was:
"Great job putting your pee in the potty! See how fast that was? Now
you can get right back to playing!" Some kids might have a hard

time understanding that they can walk away from an activity to use the potty and then return to the activity when they are done. You can demonstrate this for them on a visual schedule by showing their game or toys first, followed by a trip to the potty, and then their game or toys again as the final step. This lets them know that their playtime doesn't have to be over just because they are visiting the bathroom.

Occasionally, some children will have small dribbles in their underwear before making it to the potty, not even enough to penetrate through to make their pants wet. In most cases, this is normal and shouldn't be considered an accident. It is your child's way of testing the limits to see how long they can go before stopping and getting to the potty, or could be a result of developing interoception as your child learns their urges and cues. Remind them to stop and go as soon as they feel the need. As their muscle control and awareness improves, the behavior should diminish. If it persists for longer than a week or two, it could be a sign of an out-of-sync pelvic floor or low muscle tone. You can always reach out to your child's doctor or physical therapist for advice.

Power Struggles and Potty Resistance

I have yet to hear of a child who hasn't pushed the limits or thrown a tantrum when they didn't get their way, or when they are asked to do something they simply don't want to do. There are several reasons for this. As your child grows, develops, and matures, they begin to crave a certain level of independence and autonomy. Additionally, if your child has speech or language delays, they might exhibit outbursts because they are unable to communicate effectively. Certain disabilities might also lead to your child struggling with emotional regulation. When you pair these factors with potty training, sometimes it's a power struggle just waiting to happen. In psychology, there is a concept known as Premack's Principle that helps to put this into perspective.

This principle states that a person is likely to perform an undesirable behavior, or low probability behavior, in order to have access to something more desirable, or a high probability behavior.

Having an accident in their underwear, refusing to sit on the potty, or acting out about potty use in general is likely an undesirable behavior to your child; they don't necessarily want to do those things. But this behavior can potentially lead to them getting their diapers back, getting extra attention from you, or avoidance of having to change their routine and step outside their comfort zone, all of which are desirable things to them.

Most likely, a child who is having these struggles with potty training is not going to use the potty simply because you ask them to. There has to be something of value in it for them. Every child has a motivator, whether it be candy, toys, a special activity, TV time, or staying up late; you just have to discover what it is, and it might not necessarily be what you expect. Maybe they won't go sit on the potty for a piece of chocolate, but they will in order to get to watch a video on their tablet. If you find out their motivator, you can use it as reinforcement to encourage the behavior you want (like using the potty), then you'll both end up satisfied.

An example of this could be: "If you want to watch your TV show, you have to use the potty correctly first." In this case, the less desirable behavior of using the potty is getting them access to the more desirable behavior of watching TV.

When you encounter these power struggles after you have addressed any fears or sensory needs, and you're certain that your child understands what to do when it comes to using the potty but they continue to choose not to, you should treat it the same way as if they were acting out about anything else. In these scenarios, you have progressed from a potty training issue to a behavior issue. Many parents feel the need to, but you don't have to feel guilty or walk on eggshells about enforcing the new boundaries of using the potty.

Also keep in mind that a child's motivation for negative behavior is attention and connection from you, even if it results in a negative response. Try your best to keep your reaction to the unfavorable behaviors to a minimum and continue to put extra focus on them when they use the potty correctly. Once your child realizes that they can obtain a bigger connection with you when they use the potty, the extra effort of any unfavorable behaviors should fade quickly.

If your child repeatedly pees or poops on the floor or in their undies and you think they could be doing it purposefully, calmly and matter-of-factly restate what happened along with the expectation, "You were feeling angry and you peed on the floor. Please remember for next time that pee *only* goes in the potty." Any further reaction could unintentionally reinforce the behavior.

Offering Choices

Another amazing, yet super simple way to help avoid power struggles is to offer your child plenty of age-appropriate choices surrounding their potty use. This does not include, "Do you want to sit on the potty, or no?" but it might sound like, "It's time to sit on the potty. Do you want to use the small potty or try the toilet in mommy's bathroom?" You can also offer choices about what activity to do while they sit on the potty or what reward they will choose when they are done. When your child has a say in what's happening to them, they feel powerful and in control, and therefore you'll be less likely to encounter resistance or a power struggle over using the potty.

For children who struggle with communication, consider creating a choice board for them. This can be a printout of pictures of their different options. When it's time to use the potty, show them two different pictures and let them make their choice. The process then becomes a collaborative effort instead of something they are being forced by you to do.

Making Potty Time Fun

Playing while on the potty can make it feel less like a chore. Think of a fun game or a sensory toy that your child can hold while they sit on the potty. You can create a small basket of activities and games that you keep aside just for potty time to give your child added motivation to sit and try. These activities also provide great opportunities to offer choices.

Likewise, you can reserve a fun activity for after they are done using the potty by using a simple if/then statement. For example, "If you use the potty, then we can bake cookies!" You can even play on the way to the potty: "Let's walk like animals to the bathroom. You be a kangaroo and I'll be a bear!" or "I'll race you to the bathroom, 3-2-1, go!" Protesting is harder when you're having fun!

Potty Fear

Some children will appear to have a genuine fear of the potty, toilet, or bathroom. Additionally, they might have a fear of releasing their pee or poop without the comfort of their diapers. Important to realize is that no matter how far-fetched these fears seem to us, to your child, they are their reality. If your child refuses to enter the bathroom, screams, cries, or clings to you when near the potty, or withholds their pee and poop when diapers are off to the point of discomfort, there is a strong chance that the issue is more deeply rooted than just a simple resistance to change.

While I know it's frustrating and seems like you can't make any progress with potty training if your child won't even go into the bathroom, have some faith. There are ways to help your child come around. Believe it or not, total avoidance of the issue (which actually applies to any fear or anxiety), can validate and intensify that fear and make it last longer. But if you gently push them a little harder every few days or weeks, they will get there eventually, even if at first the effort is met with resistance.

There are multiple steps involved when it comes to potty training, so sometimes you can keep the learning moving in the right direction by simply removing the steps that frighten your child. If your child is afraid of sitting on the toilet, work on washing hands and pulling pants up and down. Gradually encourage them to get closer to the toilet each time you're in the bathroom, until they can comfortably rest their hand on the lid. Then you can move towards them sitting on your lap while you sit on the toilet, then they can sit on the toilet fully clothed with the lid down, and so on. Gently encourage them to step a little further outside their comfort zone each time. Also keep in mind that there is a lot of sensory input happening with potty use, too. Sometimes sensory issues don't pop up until the potty training phase, which can catch us off guard.

Sensory avoidance might also come across as a fear. But try to put yourself in your child's shoes to uncover the problem:

Does your child not like loud noises? Maybe they are scared of the flush. Try letting them wear noise-canceling headphones, or assure them that you'll wait to flush until they're out of the room.

Does your child avoid tags in clothing? Maybe they don't like the feeling of the elastic waistband in their new underwear. Try going up a size so it's not as tight, or letting them feel different options to see what they like best.

Does your child prefer soft surfaces? They might not like the feeling of the cold, hard toilet seat, or the bathroom tile under their feet. Try a padded toilet seat or a fuzzy rug to make them feel more comfortable.

Does your child panic while sitting on the toilet? It's possible that they feel unstable or a sensation of falling due to a retained primitive reflex. Try a seat insert that has more hip support and handles for added stability.

Finding ways to make the bathroom experience sensorily satisfying for your child might just eliminate those fears that they were experiencing. (This is explained in greater detail in Chapter 7.)

I know I just covered a lot of potential ups and downs that might be encountered when potty training your child and you might be feeling a bit overwhelmed, but remember—you've got this! I want you to be aware of these things before you get started so you can feel prepared if you happen to encounter them. Just keep your expectations realistic, and know that it's not about perfection, it's about progress and patience. As an Extra Lucky parent or caregiver, you've already got the love, strength, and courage needed to tackle the most difficult things life can throw your way. Trust your instincts, lean on the tools and tips you've learned here, and celebrate every victory, no matter how small. You're guiding your child toward an exciting new level of independence, and that's something to feel proud of. You and your child are both learning, and you'll get there together!

If at any time during this journey you feel like you need a little extra boost to keep going, don't forget to reference Taryn's mantras and meditations at the back of the book.

Chapter 11:
Sitting, Standing, and Wiping

There are two decisions that can make a huge difference in the level of mess you'll be dealing with during your potty training journey: whether your boy should sit or stand as they are first learning and, one of the final pieces of the potty puzzle, how to teach your child to wipe! This chapter will walk you through the pros and cons of your boy sitting versus standing, and how to help your child master wiping, all while keeping your bathroom (and your sanity) intact. Let's dive in—preferably not into a puddle!

Standing Versus Sitting

A super common question I often get asked by parents of boys who are physically capable of the option is whether they should sit or stand to pee when learning how to use the potty. My answer is always clear without hesitation: sit! And the reason for that is, asking your little guy to sit when they poop but stand when they pee adds excess, unnecessary confusion during an already unpredictable time. It's also better from a safety standpoint. When your son is first starting to learn how to use the potty, he may be too short to reach the toilet to pee into without standing on something. Standing up on a stepstool while trying to aim properly is a lot for a child to focus on, especially if they have a disability that affects their mobility, coordination, or balance. Sitting is simply safer overall. Another aspect to consider—and I'm looking out for you here parents—is the mess. You simply don't need the added stress and frustration of wiping the toilet, and sometimes the walls and floor, each time your child pees. Sitting on the potty won't be entirely mess-free necessarily, but it does make it much more likely that they'll get the pee into the bowl where it belongs. Bottom line—we want to keep things as simple and consistent as possible for your little man, at least until they are peeing and pooping on the potty consistently before adding in the aspect of standing to pee.

Eventually when they are a potty pro, are tall enough to reach the toilet without a step stool, and are showing an interest in standing, you can teach them. This is a place for dad or another trusted male role model to step in. Using public bathrooms where urinals are available can be good places to start introducing this skill. There are also toilet targets you can purchase to help them aim into the bowl, but a lot of people are fans of just tossing a couple pieces of cereal into the toilet.

Keep in mind that there is no harm in a boy sitting to pee. In fact, a lot of pelvic floor specialists claim sitting is a better physical position to fully void the bladder. That said, he can sit as long as he, or you, wants to. Again, this is a very personal choice, so you can do what your family feels most comfortable with.

Wiping

One thing I know crosses every parent's mind, especially once you've started potty training is.....how long am I going to be wiping bums?! As a mom myself, I hate to break the bad news—you've probably still got a long way to go. Generally speaking, and it certainly isn't always the case, girls will master wiping faster than boys because, number one, their fine motor skills develop more quickly than boys, and number two, they wipe for both pee and poop, so they have a lot more opportunities to practice.

Wiping after using the potty can be a particularly challenging skill for children with disabilities to master due to a variety of factors. Physical limitations, such as reduced fine motor skills, coordination difficulties, or limited mobility, can make the act of wiping itself difficult. Cognitive or sensory processing challenges may also impact your child's ability to understand the sequence of wiping, recognize when they are clean, or tolerate the different sensory aspects of wiping. Additionally, some children with disabilities may struggle with the concept of personal hygiene, finding it hard to remember or prioritize this step in the potty routine.

Here are some tips to help encourage this final step of potty independence:

- First and foremost, keep your expectations low. The harsh reality is, many small children aren't even physically proportioned to be able to wipe effectively. Their little arms aren't quite long enough to reach around for the proper front to back wiping technique. All you can do initially is practice. They are still going to need you to go behind them with quality checks for a while to ensure they are getting themselves nice and clean.
- For pooping, I know it can seem a little intimidating to hand your child a wipe and let them try themselves. So, before you venture that far, have your child practice in the bathtub. Spread some suds or conditioner on their bottom and let them wipe with a washcloth. This is a great opportunity to teach and practice the front to back wiping motion.
- Another fun thing to do to instill the WFR (wipe, fold, repeat) is to spread some peanut butter on a plastic doll's bottom, give them a wipe and have them practice wiping, folding, wiping, folding, etc. until nothing else comes off on the wipe and the baby doll is clean. If you don't want to use peanut butter, you can also try washable markers!
- Using wet wipes is generally recommended when your child is learning to wipe after a poop for ease of use and better hygiene. They simply clean better than dry toilet paper with less effort and less waste.

Chapter 12: Potty Training During Sleep Periods

As a certified pediatric sleep expert, this chapter has my stamp of approval! Following Allison's advice on how to support your child during night and nap potty training will be sure to create success without interfering with the great sleep foundation you've established.
-Sarah Bossio, Your Zen Baby Sleep

Deciding whether to remove diapers entirely or to keep them for naps and nighttime while focusing on daytime potty use can be a complex choice, influenced by your child's unique needs, developmental stage, and comfort levels. Do you make the leap and risk the mess by letting your child sleep without diapers? Do you continue to keep them in diapers for naps and overnight and risk sending a mixed message? Is your child even capable of staying dry while sleeping yet?

Some families might choose to remove all diapers, day and night, from the start of potty training. This approach can help create more consistency, sending a clear message that your child is transitioning out of diapers entirely and all pee and poop goes only in the potty from now on. It also prevents your child from withholding their pee and poop until they get access to their sleep diaper, which can be a difficult habit to break otherwise. While daunting to think about, removing all diapers can actually be very empowering for your child and can help them build more confidence in their abilities! However, as you might suspect, this approach can be particularly challenging, especially for children with disabilities who may take longer to recognize and respond to their body's cues; have physical symptoms such as low muscle tone, constipation, or retained primitive reflexes; or have difficulty communicating their needs during the night. For these children, nights have an increased potential for bedwetting and disrupted sleep, which can be taxing on both you and your child.

On the other hand, some families may opt to focus on daytime potty use while keeping diapers for naps and nighttime. This strategy acknowledges that potty training during sleep is more challenging and complex than daytime potty training, that bladder control during sleep often develops later, and that it can be particularly difficult for children with disabilities for various reasons. By keeping diapers during sleep, you can ensure that your child is getting the rest they need without the stress of accidents or frequent wakings. However, this approach also has its downsides. For example, it might send mixed signals to your child, leading to confusion about when they are expected to use the potty versus when it's okay to rely on a diaper. That inconsistency can make it harder for your child to fully grasp the concept of potty training, potentially prolonging the process. Additionally, keeping diapers for sleep can create a dependency on them, making it harder to transition away from them completely. While there have been no specific studies including children with disabilities or delays on this topic, other research[14] has shown that the sooner diapers are removed during sleep, the sooner nighttime continence is achieved.

It's important to keep in mind that your child might be more capable than what you give them credit for, so you have to trust in their abilities and give them the credit they deserve! Avoid shying away from nap or nighttime potty training simply because you're worried about the extra laundry. As I've discussed in prior chapters, having accidents and making mistakes is all a critical part of the learning process. If there isn't something medical or physical holding them back from being able to sleep without diapers, you can absolutely give it a try.

For some children, it can be enough to eliminate all daytime diapers across the board. If you choose to forgo diapers for naps, to help set your child up for dryness, you can have them use the potty before they get into their bed or crib, and then wake them up a few minutes before they normally would or get to them as soon as they are naturally waking up and sit on the potty first thing. Within a few days, you'll likely start seeing some progress!

If you're feeling extra ambitious and would like to remove all diapers from the start both day and night, here are some tips to help encourage nighttime dryness:

- Limit fluids after dinnertime, or about 1.5 to 2 hours before sleep. Keep in mind that you don't want to withhold fluids altogether to try and be extra proactive. Staying hydrated is actually very important for bladder function and health, so you definitely don't want your child going thirsty. If your child is a big drinker and limiting fluids in the evenings might be a problem, consider funneling their liquids throughout the day so they are getting the most in the morning and a minimal amount by bedtime.

- Set up a nighttime potty station. Keeping a small floor potty on top of a towel or waterproof pad close to your child's bed or crib will make nighttime potty visits much more manageable. You can keep the space dimly lit with a nightlight and keep a roll of toilet paper or wipes and a stack of dry clothes and sheets out just in case, too. That way no one is fumbling around in the dark but you don't need to turn on bright lights, waking everyone up completely, and you can all get back to bed as quickly as possible.

As a certified pediatric sleep expert, this is an excellent strategy to avoid any behavioral reasons to avoid bedtime. During potty training, we honor our child's request to use the potty. Sometimes, a child will realize that they can ask to go potty to avoid going to sleep (just as they may ask for one more book, more water, etc.). Having a potty station set up in your child's bedroom not only makes the potty more accessible, but also creates bedtime boundaries that you have established. They are not able to leave the room but are having their potty needs met—the best of both worlds! A potty station will help reduce the amount of bedtime protest you may see during potty training.
- Sarah Bossio, Your Zen Baby Sleep

- Sleep in a single, loose-fitting layer with an elastic waist-band. That means no onesies and no sleep sacks. This will help with urge awareness even while sleeping and it will make it much faster and easier to get your child from bed to potty if they call for help in the night.
- Perform a double void. A double void is two potty visits that are close together to ensure the bladder is as empty as possible before going to bed. You can try one potty sit at the beginning of your child's bedtime routine and another within 20 to 30 minutes just before they climb into bed.
- Do some practice runs. Remember, kids thrive on routine and predictability, and this whole sleeping without a diaper thing is brand new to them. Taking off their diaper and telling them to use the potty in the night if they need to go probably won't cut it. Instead, create a little game where your child pretends to be asleep in their bed, you tickle their belly and say, "Wake up! You need to go potty!", have them get out of bed and sit on the potty as they would in the night, and then crawl back into bed. This will help them get more familiar with what might actually go down in the night when they need to go, and it makes things fun!
- Move wake up time 15 minutes earlier. The most likely time that your child, or anyone really, needs to pee is first thing when they wake up in the morning. Until now, your child is used to waking up and releasing in their diaper right away. Try to beat them to it and get them out of bed either just before they would normally wake up or right as they are waking up to try and catch a pee in the potty to start off your day.

Crib Versus Bed

One of the most common retorts that I get when encouraging families to start nap and nighttime potty training is, "But I can't do that because my child still sleeps in a crib!" I completely understand that removing diapers for sleep is a scary enough undertaking without worrying about your child having an accident because they can't get out of their crib and onto the potty in time.

But the simple truth is, there really isn't much difference between potty training in a crib versus a bed. Your child's need for you to be active and involved in this process doesn't change! Even if your child were already sleeping in a bed, chances are they are going to need you there to help them use the potty at night, at least in the beginning. If your child is still sleeping in a crib, I would recommend putting a baby monitor in their room so they can call out if they need to use the potty. Make sure your child knows to call for you if they feel the urge to go potty while they're sleeping and test it out during the day so they know how it works. Also, if you hear stirring or fussing from their crib, it could be an indicator that they are feeling the urge but aren't quite waking up to alert you, so when you first get started, try to be ready to spring into action quickly.

All of this being said, if you had planned on transitioning your child to a big kid bed any time in the near future anyway, then definitely do that and let them adjust to the new sleeping arrangements *before* tackling potty training. Throwing too many changes at your child at one time greatly increases the chances of regressing in one or more of those new skills. But don't feel like you need to rush into transitioning to a bed just for the sake of improving nighttime potty training. There is no reason why you can't go diaper-free for naps and nighttime while your child stays comfortable and happy in their crib.

As a certified pediatric sleep consultant, this is the same advice I give to parents who are trying to decide between making the transition to the big kid bed or potty training. Both of these events are big and exciting, and being well-adjusted to the new sleep space first will only help them retain their new potty training skills when the time comes.
- Sarah Bossio, Your Zen Baby Sleep

An In-Between Approach

Some options to still prevent confusion and mixed signals, while not actively pursuing nap or nighttime potty training:

- Switch to a cloth option that feels more like your child's daytime underwear. Cloth diapers or training pants are often a good choice because they aren't quite as absorbent as diapers (which I know can defeat the purpose in some cases), but do allow more learning to take place because your child is more easily able to feel the wetness from an accident.
- You can change from diapers to disposable training underwear or switch the brand you've been using so they look very different from what your child is used to.
- To still send clear messaging and expectations, refer to all of these options as sleep or nighttime underwear so the word "diaper" is out of the conversation completely. The expectation that they should try hard to get all pee and poop in the potty is still there, but you also have that absorbency in case of accidents for added peace of mind.

Ultimately, the approach to nap and nighttime potty training should be tailored to each individual child's needs, with a focus on what will make them feel supported and successful. If you feel like your child isn't ready for nighttime potty training or like you just can't handle it right now for one reason or another, I fully support your decision!

Chapter 13: Common Challenges

As exciting as potty training can be, it's totally normal to hit a few speed bumps along the way—after all, your child's journey is going to be just as unique as they are! You might encounter everything from poop troubles to those moments when they just refuse to pee or poop altogether, with some of these challenges leaving you feeling as though you've hit a wall. The good news is you're not alone, and these hurdles are more common than you might think. In this section, I'll dive into some of the trickier aspects of potty training and share practical strategies to help you tackle them with confidence. Every challenge is an opportunity for growth!

Withholding

In the early stages of potty training, it can be fairly common for your child to pee and poop less while they are learning their body cues. Sometimes, this can be pretty worrisome—especially when it seems to go on for hours and you're wondering how they can possibly be holding it that long—but typically it's just a temporary adjustment to their normal potty routine and not something to worry about.

However, there are times where children do withhold pee and poop out of fear or resistance to using the potty. This could present in a few different ways:

- Not peeing for very long periods of time (generally several hours or more) to the point of pain or discomfort, which can sometimes result in medical complications, like constipation or urinary tract infection (UTI)
- Trying to physically hold back from releasing pee or poop when they really need to go by putting their hands over their genitals or crossing their legs

- Holding in their pee or poop until bedtime, maybe when they get access to a diaper or disposable training underwear
- Holding it in until they physically can't anymore

There are different reasons why children with disabilities resort to withholding behaviors. The first could be out of a genuine fear of the changes associated with potty training. This milestone can often be intimidating for kids, because up until this point they've only had to release their pee and poop mindlessly into their diaper where it stays nice and contained. When the diapers go away, the sensation of releasing pee or poop is very different, and even scary.

Additionally, children might resist peeing and pooping on the potty due to one thing young children are notoriously known for: the power struggle. The age that children are often ready for potty training is also the age where they begin experimenting with their autonomy, which can present itself through big emotions. The struggle of "I'm absolutely not going to poop until you give me that diaper back" can become very real.

No matter what the reason for their withholding is, it is stressful and frustrating. It makes it much harder to get pee and poop in the potty and feel like you're seeing progress when they aren't peeing and pooping at all! And then there's the larger question that we might struggle with internally: "Am I doing them physical harm by continuing this?" Don't worry though. There are ways to help your child overcome their withholding tendencies. Let's discuss.

I've mentioned this before, but remember, some children will need to pee every 30 minutes or so and others will only need to go a few times per day. Both types of potty frequencies are normal. However, you know your child best and you'll be able to tell if they really need to pee or poop but aren't making the move to do so.

When those physical signs and behavior changes become more apparent, try to remove some of the pressure and stress and make the process as fun as you can, so no matter what their reasoning is for not releasing on the potty, they at least will be super motivated to give it a try!

- Fill up a basket with new sensory toys that you know your child will love playing with and only have them accessible during potty time. Sensory toys are less stimulating than electronic devices, so it could help to distract your child while relaxing them enough to release.
- Offer appropriate choices. Choices are always a great way for your child to feel a certain level of control during an otherwise uncertain time. Let them choose how to make the environment comfortable for them. Think things like: lights on or off? Privacy or company? Sit on the toilet backwards or forwards? Sing a song or blow some bubbles?
- Speaking of blowing bubbles—this is a great way for your child to relax and release their bladder and bowels. It doesn't have to be just blowing bubbles. It could be a pinwheel, a toy trumpet, or blowing through a straw into a glass of milk. The act of blowing mimics deep breathing, which helps to relax the pelvic floor.
- Placing your child's feet into a small tub of warm water while they sit on the potty can help to release their bladder. It can also be a fun distraction for them while they sit. They can "wash" toy cars or play with toy sharks in the water. Think of it as a potty sensory bin!
- Give your child a sheet of stickers while sitting on the potty and ask them to put a sticker on each of their toes. The action of bending over can actually help massage the abdomen, making it easier to pee or poop!
- This final trick, I learned from my labor and delivery nurse after I had my son. A drop or two of peppermint oil in the toilet bowl before sitting down can trigger bladder release. I gave birth in a very busy hospital and they needed those birthing rooms. But you can't be released to recovery until you've peed! She would use this trick to help women be able to go faster and easier, and it can work during potty training, too!

But what if none of these tips or tricks work? Should you keep going? I typically encourage parents to give a solid college try for at least 3 full days to see if the withholding behaviors improve before deciding to take a break from potty training. Extreme withholding, for 12 hours or more for pee or 3 days or more for poop, can potentially lead to physical problems. And above all else, we always want to prioritize health and safety. Always listen to your gut. If it truly feels wrong to keep going, then it probably is. You can always take some time off to let your child start peeing and pooping normally again and then revisit potty training later.

Poop Problems

One of the most common struggles parents will encounter during potty training involves getting their child to poop on the potty. They may be experiencing poop accidents, withholding poop, reserving pooping until nap or nighttime, or even handling their poop, also known as fecal smearing. Understanding the underlying factors and causes that contribute to these challenges can help you and your child's caregivers to provide the necessary support and patience needed to help them navigate this delicate stage of the potty training process.

Reasons Children Struggle with Pooping on the Potty

Let's explore some of the most common reasons that children with disabilities might have a hard time pooping on the potty:

Sensory issues. Pooping in the potty versus pooping in a diaper is a very different sensation that can be hard for a lot of kids to come to terms with. When they poop in their diaper (or underwear), the poop comes out and stays right up against their body. When they poop into the potty, the poop falls out and away from their body, which can be pretty darn scary to experience the first few times. Then, factor in all of the sensory input they are getting from the bathroom environment itself, such as bright lights, cold temperatures, hard surfaces, strong odors, and loud flushes. This all can quickly lead to sensory overwhelm for some children, causing their bodies to tense up and not be able to relax and release their poop into the potty.

Past or ongoing constipation. Constipation is another common issue that can complicate potty training for children with disabilities. Many children with disabilities are more prone to constipation due to a combination of factors, such as medication side effects, dietary restrictions, or difficulties with mobility. When a child is constipated, passing stool becomes painful, and they may begin to associate using the potty with that pain or discomfort. This can create a cycle of withholding, where your child avoids going to the bathroom, leading to even more severe constipation. Some kids would prefer to just wait and release their poop when they have the comfort zone of their familiar diapers.

Physical issues such as muscle tone. Low muscle tone (hypotonia) is also a significant factor that can impact your child's ability to successfully use the potty. Children with low muscle tone may struggle to control the muscles needed for bowel movements. This lack of control can make it difficult for them to push out stool or to sense when they need to go, leading to accidents or a reliance on diapers. Additionally, low muscle tone can affect your child's posture and balance, making it uncomfortable or challenging for them to sit on the potty for extended periods of time. On the other hand, high muscle tone (hypertonia) can create stiffness and tightness in the muscles, making it difficult for your child to relax enough to empty their bladder or bowels. It may also contribute to a lack of urge awareness or constipation.

From Brittany Steidel, Doctor of Physical Therapy: Children with conditions like Down syndrome and autism often present with low muscle tone, also known as hypotonia, which affects not only their skeletal muscles but also impacts the smooth muscle in organs. Since the digestive system relies on smooth muscle function to move food through the intestines, low tone in these muscles can slow this process down, leading to an increased frequency of constipation.

Privacy concerns. Some children might feel as though some of their privacy has been taken away along with their diapers when you first start potty training. If you think about it, their body has always been covered while they pooped up to this point in their lives, which offers a nice amount of privacy. When the diapers go away and their exposed bottom hovers over the hole of a toilet or potty, they could be hesitant to poop without the comfort and privacy that being covered up can bring. This can really be a big deal for some kids, especially those who would tend to hide to poop in their diaper before potty training began.

Time to learn. Learning how to poop in the potty can take a lot longer to master because there are fewer opportunities to practice! Your child probably only poops once for every 5 to 10 pees. So in theory, it could take 5 to 10 times longer for your child to learn how to poop on the potty!

Techniques to Improve Progress

Now that I've discussed some of the most common reasons why it is more challenging for some children to poop on the potty, let's discuss some ways to overcome these challenges and start getting poop in the potty where it belongs!

We already discussed this a bit in Chapter 4, but first and foremost, you want to remove any negative language or terminology associated with poop or pooping and instead, help normalize it for your child. If your child has a positive outlook on pooping and realizes that it is healthy and something everyone does, they'll be less hesitant to poop on the potty. Talk about how cool and fascinating poop can be, how it can come out in different shapes, sizes, and even colors, and then encourage them to put their poop in the potty or toilet so they can observe it for themselves. You can also talk about how much better your body feels after you let your poop out into the potty. Poop gets a bad rap as being something gross or even taboo to talk about. Kids internalize this, leading them to think that it's something to be ashamed of or to be kept hidden. Talking about it early and opening up those conversations will shift their whole perspective!

Constipation Symptoms

Next, you will need to assess your child for constipation. Constipation can be tricky to identify, as it's not all about hard, infrequent poops. Believe it or not, there are some children that poop multiple times each day and are still constipated. Any time your child is struggling to poop during potty training, you should mention it to their doctor so that constipation can either be ruled out or treated.

Here are some symptoms that you might observe:

- The appearance of your child's stool might be large, hard, dry, or crumbly. The Bristol Stool Chart is a tool used to assess the form and consistency of stool, help-ing to evaluate bowel health. It features seven types of stool, numbered 1 to 7. Types 1-3 indicate constipation, while types 5-7 would be considered loose stools. Ideally, you should strive for type 4, at least on most days.
- Your child may have infrequent bowel movements that are painful or difficult to pass. Instead of daily bowel movements, your child might only go every 2 to 3 days, or even less frequently.
- They might have to strain to get their poop out.
- You may notice streaks of blood in the stool, which can happen due to anal fis-sures, or small tears in your child's anus from straining with large poops. These can be super painful!

There are also other less obvious symptoms of constipation:

- You may notice increased urination frequency—peeing more often—as a result of extra pressure on the bladder from an overly full rectum. UTIs can also be a sign of constipation.
- Your child might experience abdominal pain or hardness from stool sitting in the rectum for too long.
- You could notice changes in their eating and drinking habits. If your child seems to not have as much of an appetite as they usually do, it could mean constipation.

- Behavior changes can also be a symptom due to the discomfort that they are in but can't fully express or verbalize. Clinginess, anxiety, fussiness, or lethargy can start to pop up in your child when they are otherwise happy kids!

Bristol Stool Chart

focus posters

TYPE 1	Hard, separate lumps that resemble nuts; often hard to pass
TYPE 2	Lumpy and shaped like a sausage
TYPE 3	Sausage-shaped with surface cracks
TYPE 4	Smooth, soft, and shaped like a sausage or snake
TYPE 5	Soft, distinct blobs that pass easily
TYPE 6	Mushy stool with fluffy pieces and uneven edges
TYPE 7	Completely liquid with no solid parts

In some more rare and serious cases, constipation can go from minor and easily corrected to a more severe condition known as encopresis as a result of chronic, ongoing constipation. Encopresis causes the rectum to become stretched or distended and can take some time—up to a year or more—of regular bowel emptying to regain its original size and tone. Encopresis generally can be identified by streaks or smears of poop in your child's diaper or underwear. This is a sign that there could be a buildup or impaction of stool in their colon that new, softer stool is leaking around. This leakage gives the false impression that there is no way your child could be constipated because they are having multiple poops each day or their poop is very soft.

It's frustrating to deal with, but it is important to remember that any leakage isn't your child's fault, since the distention of the rectum causes a lack of urge sensitivity and therefore your child doesn't get that signal received in their brain that it's time to poop. Encopresis should always be addressed by your child's doctor. Occasionally, doctors of young children can be hesitant to diagnose constipation or encopresis, so a second opinion by a gastrointestinal specialist might be needed. Encopresis is typically diagnosed after a physical exam, or sometimes even X-rays.

Fecal Smearing

Fecal smearing, or touching and handling poop, can be a shocking and challenging behavior for parents and caregivers of children with and without disabilities. It can occur for various reasons, such as constipation or bowel impaction, which can cause discomfort and lead to digging in the anus to try and relieve pressure or physically remove stool from their body that they cannot get out otherwise. The behavior could also be simply exploratory or because your child seeks extra tactile sensory input, so they decide to handle the poop that is in their diaper or in the potty and rub it between their fingers or smear it on different surfaces. When encountering this behavior, it's important for parents and caregivers to respond in a calm, neutral way, as reacting strongly can sometimes reinforce it and make it happen more often.

To address and prevent this behavior, try to ensure that your child's sensory needs are met through alternative, more appropriate activities and textures. By providing them with clay or slime during the day, they are receiving that sensory input in other ways and will be less inclined to resort to handling their poop. Managing and preventing constipation can also help. And of course, it's important to reinforce proper bathroom habits and hygiene in a patient, consistent manner.

Correcting and Managing Constipation

Even though it makes the potty training process feel even more daunting, rest assured that most constipation is easily treatable. There are several effective ways to correct and prevent constipation, but different treatments will work better than others for everyone. Let's explore some of the options so you can discuss them with your child's doctor:

- The most common things to do across the board are to increase fluid intake—especially water if your child will drink it—and make sure they are active for at least 60 minutes each day. Activities like running, jumping, crawl-ing, and climb-ing are all great ways to engage the core and get the body in optimal physical condition to have healthy, regular poops. Obviously for children with mobility challenges, this will be more difficult, so consider speaking with their doctors and therapists for other ways to engage their muscles and increase blood flow within the abdomen.
- From a dietary standpoint, consider more "P foods." Pears, prunes, plums, papa-ya, and peas are all great examples of foods that can help pooping. Pear juice or prune juice can help more mild cases as well. Be sure your child is getting as much dietary fiber as possible. This can be really challenging, so sometimes of-fering a supplemental source of fiber is needed. HyFiber® for Kids is a great choice because it packs a lot of fiber into a very small dose, while

being made with natural ingredients, keeping it gentle for your child's digestive system and safe to use long term.

- In addition to adding fiber, you can consider incorporating pre- and probiotics, which are various strains of bacteria (good bacteria!) that help balance the gut.
- Constipation can also stem from a magnesium deficiency. Certain magnesium supplements can help increase bowel movement frequency.
- Another amazing natural remedy is bowel massage. Bowel massage helps stimulate motility and gets the poop pushed through the colon.
- Finally, medications could be needed as well. Osmotic laxatives, such as polyethylene glycol 3350, are typically recommended by pediatricians for a gentle, short-term solution to constipation. A doctor may recommend a stimulant laxa-tive, such as bisacodyl or senna, over an osmotic laxative when quicker relief is needed to stimulate bowel movements, particularly if your child is experiencing more severe constipation or has not responded well to other treatments. Occasionally, a suppository or enema could be needed when your child hasn't had a bowel movement in several days, or they are trying to go but in a lot of pain. These usually provide almost immediate results, but I try to reserve them for worst-case scenarios, as the administration can sometimes be traumatizing for all involved, setting back your progress even further. If you decide that a medi-cal intervention is the route you need to go to treat your little one's constipation, always be sure to consult with their doctor first to get the best plan in place for your child's specific needs.
- When there is a bowel impaction or encopresis, generally your doctor will have you perform a bowel cleanout using high doses of osmotic or stimulant laxa-tives over the course of a few days' time.

- Occasionally, bowel retraining is also required, which involves sitting your child on the potty for a few minutes after meals in order to encourage regular bowel movements and prevent withholding. Pediatric pelvic floor physical therapy may also be needed in some cases.

Pro-tip from Taryn: As a mom of four, we have had our share of digestive issues. Mom friends in the disability community introduced me to HyFiber® for Kids years ago, and it was the first thing that consistently got my daughters back on track, and the first product I turn to in these scenarios.

Activities to Reduce Constipation

By Brittany Steindl, DPT, BLS Physical Therapy
Pediatric Physical Therapist

Core and Abdominal Strengthening	Exercises like belly breathing, bridging, and child-friendly yoga poses (such as the "cat-cow" or "happy baby" pose) strengthen the core muscles, supporting the abdominal region and promoting healthy bowel movements.
Daily Physical Movement	Encourage activities like walking, running, or jumping, which promote natural muscle engagement and stimulate the digestive system. For younger children, setting up obstacle courses or simple movement games can be fun and beneficial.
Gentle Abdominal Massage	Perform a gentle circular massage on the child's abdomen, moving clockwise, which can stimulate the intestines. This massage, often done with light pressure, can be especially helpful after meals to encourage bowel movement.
Routine Bathroom Times	Setting a consistent time for the child to sit on the toilet, ideally after meals, can help establish regular bowel habits and take advantage of the body's natural post-meal digestive reflex.
Hydration and Fiber-Rich Foods	Encourage water intake throughout the day and fiber-rich foods, like fruits, vegetables, and whole grains, to keep stools soft and promote ease of bowel movements.
Squatting Positions	Utilize a small stool (like a Squatty Potty®) under the child's feet during bathroom time, which mimics a squatting position. This helps straighten the rectum, facilitating easier bowel movements.

You'll want to be sure that you give your child plenty of time to heal after an episode of constipation before expecting them to put their poop in the potty. I generally recommend a recovery period of about 30 days of regular poops before pressing forward with this aspect of potty training. So, you can either continue to allow your child to use a diaper for pooping or let them poop however they feel most comfortable, allowing their body to return to optimal physical condition.

Eventually, the goal is to move away from diapers and get your child pooping in the potty or toilet. Once they seem to be pooping more regularly and their constipation is resolved, as well as having a more positive outlook on pooping in general, you can start thinking about shifting the expectations again. That means, counting down the days to pooping in the potty and saying goodbye to the diapers again for good. It's very important to give your child advance notice of the upcoming changes to their potty habits so they have time to mentally prepare, and so that you are able to provide them with the proper reassurance and empowerment needed to tackle this challenging part of the process! Be sure to be patient and understanding, allowing them to ask questions and voice concerns over pooping on the potty. Take a few days to start talking about poop more in your daily conversations, reading books about it together, and overall just bringing poop positivity without putting pressure on them to change anything themselves too quickly. This is a sensitive issue and you don't want to push your child too hard.

Here are some easy, practical things to do while helping your child learn how to poop on the potty:

- If your child was one to seek privacy for pooping before potty training started, you can create a private and comfortable space for them to use the potty, such as setting up a "poop tent" or using a small potty in their favorite hiding spot. If your child already only uses the toilet, to help maintain some privacy, wrapping them in a blanket can help. Additionally, allowing some alone time while they sit on the potty can also make them feel more at ease. You can pretend to have forgotten something in the other room for a minute or two while your child sits and be surprised with a success when you come back!

- Using a small distraction during potty time can help your child relax and focus long enough to poop. Choose a new, engaging activity that's reserved only for poop attempts, like fidget or sensory toys, rather than screen time, which can be overly distracting and lead to power struggles. Keeping these activities in sight but out of reach can also motivate your child. But ensure they don't sit for too long—if they haven't pooped within five to seven minutes, it's best to take a break and try again later.

- A practical and effective way to help children relax on the potty is by engaging them in activities that involve blowing, such as blowing bubbles or a pinwheel. Blowing helps with pelvic floor muscle coordination, which is crucial for pooping. Since children may not fully grasp the concept of deep breathing, you can use a fun exercise like the "Flower & Candle" method. Have them inhale deeply by "smelling" a flower and then exhale by "blowing out" a candle. You can make some simple props out of paper and craft sticks to keep in the bathroom, and this playful approach turns breathing into a functional activity that supports successful pooping.

- Use rewards! Rewards should be something special and motivating, reserved exclusively for successful potty poops. Offering rewards immediately after the act helps reinforce the connection between the behavior and the prize. Over time, as the habit becomes more ingrained, rewards can be phased out.

- Ensure your child has proper posture while sitting on the toilet, with feet flat, knees above hip level, and a slight forward lean. This position mimics a natural squat, making it easier for them to poop without straining. If their feet dangle or they use their hands to push up for support, it can make pooping more difficult, leading to reluctance or constipation. Using a Squatty Potty® can help your child easily achieve this posture. For kids who prefer to stand or lie down to poop, you'll want to encourage them to practice squatting and sitting in the correct position during the day to help them get comfortable with using the potty.

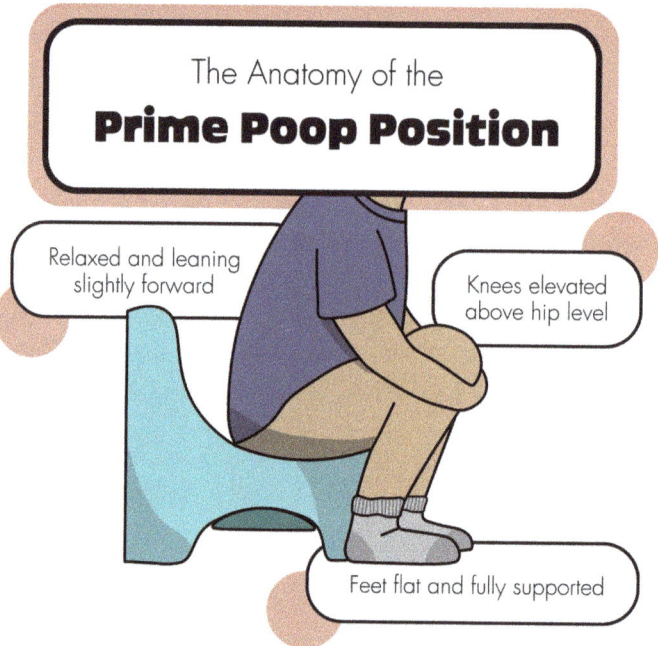

The Anatomy of the
Prime Poop Position

Relaxed and leaning slightly forward

Knees elevated above hip level

Feet flat and fully supported

Commitment and consistency are key to achieving poop success, which I've talked a lot about throughout this entire book. There is no miracle cure, but these practical implementations should help you identify where the problem is coming from and start to see progress almost immediately. Progress isn't necessarily only poop going in the potty. Progress will look like:

- your child having more regular, consistent bowel movements without pain or discomfort
- your child being more open to talking about poop and pooping
- you changing your verbiage when talking to them about poop
- less resistance when sitting on the potty for a poop attempt

All of these little things will build up to that end goal you've been waiting for: your child pooping in the potty on their own, every time. Try to find those small successes and focus on them so you know you are moving in the right direction.

Regressions

Say your child has been doing great with using the potty. They no longer need reminders, they are pooping consistently, they're even staying dry overnight sometimes! Life is good. Then, out of nowhere, it's one accident after another and it seems like everything they previously learned went out the window! This is what would be classified as a potty training regression.

What Is a Potty Training Regression?

A regression in any aspect is when a child reverts back to a previous stage of behavior or development. As I've mentioned throughout the book, kids are creatures of habit, and they thrive on routines and predictability. So regressions are usually observed when kids are feeling emotional stress as a result of some sort of disruption to their regular routine. Very young children, or children with speech or language delays, can't always express their emotions clearly, so instead, they may regress to a time where they remember feeling more safe and secure as a way to seek comfort or extra attention from you as a type of defense mechanism. For many children, that safety and security comes through the intimacy of having their diaper or clothing changed by a parent or caregiver, and that can lead to them having more potty accidents. Falling into a potty training regression is a child's way of saying, "Help me. I'm feeling out of sorts and I need extra love and attention from you right now."

These regressions can come in the form of having more accidents during the day, no longer self-initiating potty use, wetting themselves during nap or nighttime when they were previously dry, or no longer pooping in the potty. No matter how it presents itself, it obviously leads to a lot of frustration and uncertainty as a parent! Believe it or

145

not, potty training regressions are fairly common. That said, it doesn't make it any less difficult or frustrating, for either you or your child.

Causes of Regressions

Regressions can sometimes happen as a result of a medical issue such as constipation or a UTI, so it is always important to get those causes ruled out first. Sometimes children with disabilities will have a hard time expressing pain or discomfort, so a regression might seem behavioral when it is actually not in your child's control at all.

If there is nothing medical going on, it's likely that the regression stems from some sort of emotional stress. The likelihood of a regression occurring often depends on the amount of time that separates the stressful event and the start of potty training. Basically, the longer your child has been fully potty trained, the less likely they are to experience a potty training regression. This is why it is typically recommended that there be at least an eight-week buffer period between other major changes and the start of potty training to give your child a chance to adjust to one transition before moving on to another.

Here are some common non-medical causes of potty training regressions:

- moving to a new home
- starting school for the first time or moving to a new school
- changes in caregivers or therapists
- a new baby joining the family and being promoted to big sibling status
- an injury or illness
- parents divorcing
- the death of a loved one

But smaller changes can also cause regressions. It all depends on how sensitive your child is to change, and how well they are able to cope with those changes. Sometimes, things that would seem insignificant to us, like a parent going away for a business trip, can still be enough to trigger potty setbacks.

School and Potty Training Regressions

Let's talk a little bit about school specifically and why that can cause potty regressions.

- If your child is starting school for the first time, it is a totally new environment for them to get used to. It's different from home in so many ways. Not only is the space different, but the people they are with are different. Maybe they only felt comfortable going to the potty for mom or dad. Now that mom or dad aren't there, what are they supposed to do? That uncertainty can lead to accidents in the classroom.
- They might not feel comfortable telling someone else that they need to use the potty, especially in front of a group of their peers, or they might not be able to communicate that need to someone else effectively.
- They might have anxiety about the toilet being different from what they're used to at home, or the bathroom being a larger space, or more noise. It's important to view the new bathroom from your child's perspective and consider any sensory challenges they might encounter.
- The extra noise and activity in the classroom can lead to them being too distracted, not allowing them to be able to pay attention to their body urges and cues that their bladder is full or that they need to poop. Overstimulation can also lead to accidents because they get fatigued, both mentally and physically, throughout the course of the school day.
- Being at school is likely a whole different schedule than what your child was used to at home. Things are more regimented—maybe potty visits are at set times throughout the day instead of just whenever they feel the need to go. The times they are eating and drinking may also be different, which throws off the timing or frequency in which they tend to pee or poop.

- Your child might encounter unfair expectations. Are they expected to self initiate, go into the bathroom and undress, potty, redress, flush, and wash hands all on their own? Are they expected to sit on the potty during set potty times, even when they don't really need to go or want to stop what they're doing?

These are all things to keep in mind so that you can be set up to help your child through the transition of starting or returning to school after leaving the diapers behind.

How to Handle a Regression

If your child experiences a potty training regression, it's important not to panic. Start by identifying the cause, whether it's medical or related to stress. If stress is the culprit, focus on maintaining a consistent routine, as predictability helps children adjust. As tempting as it may be to maintain your sanity, avoid reverting back to diapers, as this could signal a lack of confidence in your child's ability. Do your best to stay the course and bring your confidence and reassurance to the table on their behalf.

Here are some ways to manage a potty training regression and help your child get back on track:

- Offer emotional support by spending quality one-on-one time with your child each day to help them feel secure and connected. Make sure it is truly quality time, even if it is only a few minutes. No distractions, no phones, no other sib-lings, just you spending time with your child engaged in an activity of their choice. This will help them fill their attention tanks with other things besides the attention they would get from having an accident, and they'll naturally lean to-ward the positive attention instead of resorting to those negative behaviors.
- You can even turn potty time into a time of connection, where you read your child a special story, sing a song, or play a game together while they go. This can replace the

attention they were getting from having an accident.

- Your child might need some extra reminders from you to use the potty during this time if they are preoccupied with a change that has been going on. Prompting them to use the potty during times when they would typically need to go, or during transitions when it makes sense to work into the day easily, can help your child avoid accidents and reestablish their potty habits.

- Your child can also benefit from receiving a small reward when they show good potty habits to reinforce the proper behavior. If the use of rewards helped when you first potty trained your child, try bringing those back temporarily to help your child get back on track.

- Stay positive and patient, celebrating any small successes and responding calmly to accidents. Focus on the positive behaviors your child exhibits instead of the accidents. Consistency, support, and positivity are key to helping your child get back on track.

How Long Will It Last?

Typically, regressions are only very temporary (in the scheme of things, even though it feels like an eternity when you're living it!), and within a couple weeks, they will be back on track. Generally speaking, the longer a child has been potty trained means the less likely they are to have a regression and the shorter it will be. If you just finished potty training, or at least thought you did, a few weeks ago as opposed to several months ago, a regression is more likely and may last a little longer.

For the most part, potty regressions are harmless and temporary. However, if you notice that your child seems to be physically or emotionally affected by the regression, or if the regression persists for longer than a few weeks, try reaching out to your doctor to be sure there isn't something deeper going on. It's rare, but sometimes going back to diapers can help everyone recover from the stress associated with a regression so you can start potty training over again with a clean slate after some time has passed.

Potty training regressions can be tough, but try to see things from your child's perspective—change can be overwhelming for them. Stay calm, supportive, and positive. Focus on taking it one day at a time, and remember that your child is capable and will get back on track soon.

Lack of Self-Initiation

Another common struggle that parents encounter during potty training is a lack of self-initiation. This includes your child not telling you when they need to go or having accidents if you're not the one guiding them to the potty. Learning to listen to their body and either going to the potty themselves or letting you know they need the bathroom is a crucial skill in potty independence. So, it can be understandably frustrating when this piece of the puzzle seems to be missing. At times, it might feel like you're the one who's potty trained—constantly monitoring the clock and your child's cues to prevent accidents. But, as with all aspects of potty training, it's important to remember that every child's journey is different.

For many children, especially those with speech or communication delays, self-initiation can be one of the last skills to click into place. And this can be even more pronounced in children with disabilities. Children with developmental, physical, or sensory challenges might have a harder time recognizing the signals their body is sending them. This doesn't mean they won't learn—it just means they might need different strategies and more time.

Visual supports, like picture schedules or social stories, can be incredibly helpful for children who struggle with self-initiation. These tools give them clear, consistent reminders about what to do when they feel the urge to go. Scheduled potty times are another effective strategy, particularly for children who might not yet recognize when they need to go. By determining approximately how often they naturally need to use the potty and taking them to the potty around those times, you're helping them start to experience what a full bladder feels like paired with the relief of having emptied it, which can eventually lead to better self-initiation.

It's also important to acknowledge that some children, due to their unique needs, may never be able to fully self-initiate their potty use. And that's perfectly okay. Progress looks different for every child, and what matters most is finding what works for your child and your family. If success for your child means going potty on a schedule or you reading their cues and helping them to the bathroom, then that is a huge win in itself.

We've already touched on the importance of not over-prompting your child, as this can slow down their learning process. The goal is for your child to learn what a full bladder feels like so their brain gets the chance to send the signal, "Take me to the potty!" If they're taken too frequently before they truly need to go, that connection might not develop properly. While it might seem counterintuitive, allowing your child to have accidents can actually be a crucial part of their learning for this phase. It might mean more cleanup initially, but it speeds up their understanding of their body's signals, which is the key to self-initiation.

If your child is struggling with recognizing when they need to go, try to help them connect the dots. For instance, if you notice your child dancing around but not heading to the potty, you could say, "Hey, I see you've got some wiggles. That's your body telling you it's potty time! Let's go sit." Over time, you can encourage more independence by asking, "I'm noticing the wiggles again! What's your body telling you?" This helps them start to take responsibility for their needs, with your support and encouragement.

Offering occasional reminders can also be helpful, especially when your child is deeply engaged in play or another activity. A simple, "Remember, when you need to go potty, it's right here," can keep the idea fresh in their mind without being intrusive.

And when you're out and about, practice makes perfect. Familiarizing your child with bathrooms in new places can reduce anxiety and prevent accidents. You might even offer them a choice, like using a bathroom in the store or a travel potty in the car, to give them a sense of control.

While these challenges can feel super overwhelming when you're living them, they're just another part of the process—and remember, you're more than capable of handling anything that gets thrown your way. With a little patience, the right strategies, and a positive mindset, you'll find your way to the finish line. Trust yourself and know that you're doing an amazing job guiding your child toward success, but also don't forget about your support system! You can always get advice from the professionals on your care team, or reach out to a potty training expert such as myself for additional guidance if you feel like you need it. I always say, asking for help shows strength, not weakness!

When to Press Pause

Potty training can be a journey filled with ups and downs, especially when your child has a disability. There may be times when you feel like you're facing more struggles than successes, or it even feels like you're moving backward. It's completely natural to start questioning if your child is truly ready or if the time is right. Maybe you're thinking about hitting pause and trying again later, and that's always allowed! It's important to listen to your gut in combination with signs you're seeing from your child, without feeling any guilt or hesitation about taking a break.

Breaks during potty training, especially when justified, are not setbacks but opportunities for both your child and you to grow and regroup.

If you're on the fence about whether to keep going or take a step back, consider if any of these signs of unpreparedness might be present:

A genuine fear of the potty itself. You might notice your child kicking, screaming, or clinging tightly when it comes time to sit on the potty, even after gentle attempts to introduce the potty and bathroom in a low-pressure way.

A fear of peeing or pooping without a diaper. Some children get upset when they feel the sensation of peeing or pooping while not wearing a diaper, or they might try to hold it in to avoid going altogether.

Extreme withholding behaviors. Your child might consistently avoid going to the bathroom for very long periods of time, even to the point of pain or discomfort after holding it for hours.

Minimal or no success after several days of trying. If you've been at it consistently for a few days with little to no progress, or if things seem to be getting worse instead of better, it might be time to consider a pause.

The process seems to be negatively impacting your child's or your own mental health. Sometimes there is so much stress from potty training that it starts to mentally wear you or your child down to the point of affecting your relationship with each other or interfering with successfully executing other daily activities or tasks. If this goes on for too long, that would be a good indication that a reset is in order. If any of these situations apply, pressing pause and returning to diapers temporarily could be the best choice for you both. And please remember—this decision is not a reflection of your effort or your child's abilities! Your child's emotional readiness for potty training is a tricky thing to predict. You often won't know the timing isn't quite right until you're in the middle of it, and that's very common. Let me reassure you that taking a break is not a sign of failure. You can always come back to it when the timing feels right, or you start to notice your child maturing in other ways.

However, there are also behaviors that, while challenging, may not necessarily mean your child isn't ready for potty training, unless, of course, it's just too much for you to handle at the time.

These might include:

- Your child having an understanding of the potty's purpose but occasionally re-fusing or choosing not to use it.
- Your child having accidents at specific times, like when they don't want to stop playing or are seeking your attention.
- Your child having tantrums or meltdowns around potty use, despite them having previous success and demonstrating capability.

Potty training is known for creating power struggles, so if you encounter any of these more minor behavioral bumps, don't feel guilty about setting some boundaries and staying consistent with your expectations. These moments can be tough, but sticking to your plan and reinforcing the routine will help them pass more quickly. Consistency will be your greatest ally as you and your child work through these challenges. I'll use this opportunity to repeat that potty training is a process, not a one time event! For some families, potty training can last weeks, months, or even years, with multiple starts and stops in between before getting to an endpoint that everyone is satisfied with. You and your child are both doing amazing things by tackling this important milestone together!

Carly and M: Four Years Later, Never Looking Back

I don't care what anyone thinks—potty training is not for the faint of heart. I don't believe anyone when they say," Oh, it was so easy!" We need to be real with ourselves: it is not easy! And that is OK!

Around M's first birthday, we started to notice developmental delays, so following his lead became pivotal in his growth and for our sanity. M received an autism spectrum disorder and receptive/expressive language disorder diagnosis at 22 months old. Shortly after that, M started to show what we thought were the beginning signs he may be ready to potty train. Going "pee on potty" was a much faster process than "poop push," as M would so lovingly refer to both. It just took a long time—nearly four long years.

M would take his pull-up diaper off as soon as it was soiled. At that time, he had very little verbal communication and we were still learning how to communicate with him. I started to ask friends what potty training methods they'd tried, including what worked and what did not, but quickly realized none of those tips would be of use to us. Then it hit me to ask the person I rely on for everything—my mom! As we were navigating our new normal with M's diagnosis, she was my rock, my therapist, my research woman and everything in between. She always has the answers, so I knew she would have the golden ticket on how to potty train M. Her advice was so simplistic that I couldn't believe I didn't think of it on my own: let him be naked! Between knowing his distaste for a soiled diaper and the rewards I'd purchased for his anticipated successes, we figured we were set. I was going into this with such confidence!

155

I had taken a week off from work to fully dedicate to potty training without distractions and interruptions, though by the end of the second day, I was done. My highly stressful job was a walk in the park compared with the two days of potty training M. I knew he was a smart kid, but the brains behind how he avoided using the potty and still going was brilliant and frustrating all at the same time. Every single time M needed to go, he would sneak away and find his pull ups, put them on and go. At first, he'd bring me to his pull up and try to walk me through putting it on him. I would bring him to the toddler-sized potty, but he was not having it. He then got sly with it: he would get the pull up, put it on, and then find me so I could see him in the pull up and do his business right there! I started to hide the pull ups, but he always found them. At that point, he was then hiding in various places around the house—behind a door, drapes, and sometimes he would even go into the bathroom and close the door to go. Strangely, he had no accidents on the floor; he would control himself until he found his pull up. By the third day, he was back in pull ups full time and my confidence had taken a nosedive.

Over time, we tried our best to sporadically potty train, and it slowly started to work. At first, we would introduce the potty at home with a "no pressure" mindset. If he sat, great! If he wanted to stand in front of the toilet, great! Sometimes he went and sometimes he didn't, but we did not put any pressure into this process.

At around age 4, with the help of our private ABA team and M's teacher, we collectively decided we needed to buckle down and begin potty training with a consistent schedule. M thrived on structure and consistency, so we started to introduce the potty every hour. As the hour approached, his teacher would ask him if he had to go to the bathroom, showing him a yes/no board to help him answer. He seemed to love the bathroom, so we got lots of yesses. He would decide if he wanted to sit or stand, and he gradually started to "pee on potty"! The most exciting part of this was that he "peed on potty" his first go around in school! If he did select "no" on the hour mark, we would take that time as a sensory break opportunity, and he would take a walk, typically toward the bathroom. The question was asked again, showing the yes/no prompt.

Consistency was key, and no matter where we were—out to dinner, at an activity or at home—we introduced the potty every hour. Then magic happened! He started to "pee on potty" consistently! We had the data to prove he was going and that his pull up was dry for longer stretches throughout the day. Around 6 months later, we officially took away the pull up. He was in potty training underwear! That was a huge win for M—he felt like such a big boy! Within 2 months of that, he was fully out of pull ups, except when it came to "poop push." He was sleeping through the night in underwear, and it was such a sweet victory.

Fast forward to 2022, I was now pregnant with my second child and M was nearly 6 years old. I refused to deliver my daughter with M still in a pull up to "poop push," and he needed to be fully potty trained before her November debut. We put a step stool in front of the potty so he could rest his feet and to help push. We purchased a dozen different potty toilet seat options: ones that went over an actual toilet, ones that were child versions of a toilet. You name it, we tried it!

M's ABA therapist, A, was confident we could get M to "poop push" on the potty, so we reset the clock. It was Day One and I cannot tell you the details of what led up to that moment, but I was 8 months pregnant with a very large belly. My adrenaline was in overdrive, as was A's, and this was going to happen. We had a little potty set up in the bathroom and he had not pooped in 24 hours. For a child who was very regular, we knew he needed to go, and we seized the moment! M kept his pull up on and as he started to squat in the bath-room to "poop push," in one quick swoop, we ripped off the pull up and put him on the little potty. Getting him to sit was a challenge, but he did it, with the help of some Play-Doh in his hands to fidget with. And then it happened! With a little bit of whining and grunting in his voice, he hunched his back and planted his feet on the ground. Then he said, "poop push" and saw what was happening—he saw himself pooping! He continued to hype himself up and in his sweetest little voice, "poop push" was on repeat! We stayed as quiet as possible so he could have his moment—a moment nearly four years in the making.

Between this moment and all the pregnancy hormones, I cried the happiest tears and hugged M as tight as I had ever hugged him. He felt the joy and excitement of what he had accomplished and gave us the biggest smile, followed by, "I did it!" He was basking in this moment and knew it was a huge win. Within the next few weeks, he had transitioned from the potty training toilet to the regular bathroom one. He started to go at school, if he needed to, and there were almost no accidents.

To this day, M still uses "pee on potty" or "poop push" phrases when he needs to use the bathroom, whether it be at school, at home or when we are out in the community. It was a long four years, but that win in September 2022 was oh-so-sweet!

FINDING YOUR FLOW

Integration

Chapter 14:
Potty Training On the Go

Potty training is already a big adventure, and when you think about venturing out of the house for the first time without that comfort and security of diapers, it can feel even more daunting. Having a child with disabilities often means extra outings to various doctor's appointments or therapies on top of the typical school or daycare schedule, playdates, and family events. Whether you're navigating unfamiliar public restrooms with mobility challenges or dealing with sensory overload, it's all about finding that balance between preparation and flexibility.

Get Back out There

One of my many mantras that I will state repeatedly is: "Don't be held hostage by potty training!" Potty training is something that should, for the most part, fit seamlessly into your existing routine. You shouldn't have to change your whole life around in order to accommodate potty training! There are a lot of potty training methods out there that require being at home for a specified period of time, and frankly, with our busy lifestyles today, that's just not realistic. Also, have faith that your child is capable. They're going to need to learn how to use the potty, both in and out of the home eventually, so it's actually ideal to get out of the house and back into your usual routine as soon as possible once potty training has begun, usually after only a day or two. Not only will it help your child to have some practice being diaper-free in environments other than home, but it will also prevent any stress or anxiety from disrupting the typical schedule that they are accustomed to.

Start with some low-key activities to test the waters. Try walking around the neighborhood, if this is accessible to you, or having a picnic in the backyard. Since this outing is the first time your child will have ventured out of the house without the security and comfort of a diaper, you'll want to set them up for success as much as possible. Avoid going somewhere in the car or on public transportation at first, and also avoid super stimulating environments with a lot of distractions. Try to plan the first few outings for right after your child has used the potty and only stay out of the house for about 30 or 40 minutes. If they're able to make it through without an accident, offer lots of praise for keeping their clothes dry when you get back. If they do have an accident, that's okay, too. Staying close to home will make it easier to get back for a quick cleanup.

Over the next few days, or as soon as you feel brave enough, you can start trying outings in the car, too. Ultimately you are building up to being able to be out and about just like you used to when your child was wearing diapers. Also, keep in mind that most kids with disabilities thrive with a predictable daily routine. For many children, that could mean going back to school or a caregiver's house while their parents return to work after the weekend. And with the right preparations in place, combined with a consistent plan for all caregivers to follow (see Chapter 15), this transition can be smoother than you might expect.

When you start to go out for longer periods of time, or further distances from home, it's helpful to take a travel potty along for the ride, if your child is able to safely use one. A lot of children won't feel comfortable using public bathrooms right off the bat (even many adults still don't!) or they might not have the control needed at first to hold it long enough to get to a place that has bathroom access.

When shopping for a travel potty, mainly think about portability (Is it easy to take along with you?) and stability (Is your child going to be safe while using it?).

There are a lot of great travel potty options out there. You can decide what works best for your situation based on your child's size, comfort level, and mobility.

- If your child uses a seat insert on top of the toilet at home, to keep things con-sistent, you can always throw that in a bag to bring along with you.
- For a more discrete choice, you can get a folding seat insert that easily fits in-side your existing diaper bag.
- There are also options that can be used as a standalone potty in the back of your car, in the parking lot at the playground, or set up on the floor in the stall of a public bathroom.
- For proper positioning and posture while on the toilet, you can consider bringing along a foldable step stool to provide your child with foot support while they sit.

Pro-tip from Taryn: *One of my big stressors about potty train-ing my daughter with Down syndrome was that she has three busy older sisters and we are always on the go! Having The Jool Baby® travel potty in my trunk and their foldable potty seat in my bag were great, inexpensive investments that helped us stay on track during softball season, at the mall, or wherever we went with her sisters.*

Whichever option you decide to go with, practice with the travel potty at home before attempting to use it while you're out and about. You don't want your child's first exposure to it to be during a time of distress when they really need to go but aren't sure about this new contraption they've never seen before. Also be sure to let your child know you have it, and show it to them before leaving the house or once you're in the car so they know it is available for them to use if needed. To ease into using public bathrooms, when you get to a new place, point out where the bathrooms are at that place and offer to let them check it out if they're curious. Kids don't always realize there are bathrooms everywhere, which can cause them to hold it too long and have an accident. Low pressure exposure to these new environments will help ease any anxieties or fears they might have.

Instead of diving right into pottying in public restrooms, if your child seems hesitant, start off by introducing them to bathrooms in other familiar places besides home. Bathrooms in family members' or friends' homes, or the bathroom at school can be safe spaces. From there, you can move to family style or single-stall type bathrooms in public places, such as the library, grocery store, or mall, and then slowly acclimate them to regular multi-stall bathrooms by inviting them in to explore, without putting any pressure on them to actually go. If you go first to demonstrate, it can help them get on board and be willing to try, too.

For children with disabilities, public bathrooms can be really overwhelming from a sensory standpoint. Be sure to take any sensory sensitivities into account to avoid an unpleasant experience that can potentially set back progress. Consider packing noise-canceling headphones to help with the loud noises, or sunglasses to help with overly bright lights. Any way you can mimic the bathroom environment at home to keep things consistent and predictable will be helpful.

Bonus tip: *Use disposable toilet seat liners in between your seat insert and the toilet, or underneath travel potties on the floor, for easy clean up!*

The Potty Training Survival Kit

To give yourself some added confidence venturing out of the house without diapers, you can easily convert your current diaper bag into a "Potty Training Survival Kit." Basically all you have to do is swap out diapers for extra underwear and other changes of clothes, add in the travel potty you've chosen, the rewards you've been using at home, any extra supplies your child might need to help with sensory challenges, and you're all set!

- A few creative items to also include in this kit would be:
- Hand sanitizer to prevent prolonged restroom visits or using loud hand dryers. I like to call it "special soap," which adds an element of fun and whimsy.
- Old absorbent cloths or rags to help soak up accidents if needed. I actually like to hang onto a few old burp cloths for this purpose.
- The diaper disposal bags you used to use can help keep anything wet or soiled separate from the dry stuff until you can get home to wash it, or you can invest in an inexpensive, reusable wet bag.
- A small pack of sticky notes to cover up the sensor on the automatic flush on public toilets. This can help to avoid a potentially traumatizing bathroom expe-rience for your child. If that sensor is covered with the sticky note, the toilet won't flush until you're ready. As I'm sure you've experienced at some point yourself, occasionally the toilet can flush while you're still sitting, which can be very scary for some kids.
- You also might want to pack a spare shirt for yourself. If your child has an accident and you need to quickly scoop them up and head to the bathroom, some of that pee or poop could end up on you, too. (I speak from experience here!)

Many parents would agree that Murphy's Law applies to potty training. If you have it, you won't need it. If you don't have it, you'll definitely need it! Being prepared with all the supplies you could possibly need while you're out will make things go a lot more smoothly and give you some extra confidence!

Elena and Hope: Toileting as Communication

Potty training wasn't really on my radar until we were going through the process of transferring Hope's Early Intervention Individualized Family Service Plan (IFSP) to a public school Individualized Education Program (IEP). When I noted that Hope was still in diapers, our case manager stated clearly it would not be a barrier to her entering public school. But that exchange planted a seed in me. Between my two children—Hope has Down syndrome and Henry has upper limb differences—I've researched countless medical issues and interventions, so certainly I could take on potty training. To begin, I'd have to read up.

A lot of what I found in my research was discouraging. Most children with intellectual disabilities weren't expected to potty train until they were in elementary school, and here Hope was at two-and-a-half years old, and I, her mom, considering toileting when she had only just learned how to walk and was still taking milk from a bottle. I bounced the idea off of our many therapists and educators, all of whom gently told me to not rush things, that we had time. They did not believe Hope was ready.

When I shared the exciting news that we were embarking on potty training with our then developmental pediatrician, she spoke without a beat something along the lines of, "Why bother? It's too early. You're just going to have to do it again." My heart sank into my belly. I knew Hope could do this. What ever happened to "Mom knows her child best"? Discouragement quickly turned to defiance and, needless to say, we no longer see this physician.

Without a doctor to guide us, during a deep internet dive I stumbled on a resource from the National Down Syndrome Society about potty training readiness.[15] The handout explained that children with Down syndrome will not show readiness in the same way as their typically developing peers, and that language and fine motor skills should not be prerequisites to toileting. The handout instructed to keep the child in a pullup and check regularly for wetness to see if there were patterns to when the child used their diaper and if there were extended periods of dryness each day.

After just a few days, the patterns were crystal clear. Hope was staying dry for about 1.5 to 2 hours and wetting and soiling around the same times each day. And so, we began our journey.

My first task as potty training mom extraordinaire was to take her shopping for a little potty. She was wearing 18-24 month clothing, which I share simply to illustrate her petite size, so getting her up onto a standard toilet seemed daunting. We picked up a white plastic potty that looks like a standard toilet, complete with flusher and flushing sound. We also got an Elmo potty book with songs so practical that we still sing them to this day.

Following Hope's wet/dry schedule, I put her on the potty, and I'll never forget the precious sounds of those first little dribbles pitter-pattering into the plastic receptacle beneath her naked bottom. I'd done it! I'd potty trained my child on the first go!

Nope.

Although she'd put some pee in the potty, she was never completely emptying her bladder and shortly after would wet her pullup. We repeated the process day after day until I read that I should be putting my child in cotton underwear. And oh, those adorable cotton undies! But then came the floods...

I would find my sweet baby girl, sitting in front of her mirror, splashing in toddler glee on the hardwood floor of the playroom. (We'd already learned the hard way to roll up our rugs through this process!) What was happening??? She had extended stretches of dryness in a pullup but was wetting in cotton underwear. This meant that her accidents probably weren't even accidents at all, which means she was in full control of her little bladder. A very helpful datapoint!

If this wasn't all getting strange enough, now it was time to poop. You know how it's said that the first being a baby bird sets its eyes on imprints as its mother? Well in a similar way, the first person Hope ever pooped with became a pooping partner for life, or at least her life thus far. My husband helped her stay on her training potty at poop time by giving her a giant, daddy bear hug, and the rest is history. Six years later, occasionally she'll poop with me, but she's more inclined to hold it in until her daddy comes home from work. Sometimes being the preferred parent isn't all it's cracked up to be!

So Hope went off to school at age three in her pullups. I insisted she was potty trained and just felt no incentive to stay dry without her pullups on, but school staff doubted my information and made her a toileting plan. Preverbal, they taught her to sign "toilet" in American Sign Language, which is simply signing the letter "t" and shaking it. They also used a visual timer to prompt her to ask to visit the bathroom. So although I say she was potty trained at age two-and-a-half, school would probably say three. Potato, po-tah-to.

Once the training part of potty training is complete, then comes living with a small child who uses a toilet, and for us it wasn't as "complete" or straightforward as it sounds. We have and continue to encounter some interesting things since Hope has been potty trained, mostly surrounding using toileting as communication. During a period of later-realized emotional and physical trauma in school, she was withholding, coming home dry, sometimes in physical agony. She was trying to tell us she was scared, but it took us time to catch on to her signals. On another occasion after transitioning to kindergarten, she was having accidents at school, and only at school. After weeks of appointments that included testing her for urinary tract infections and Type I Diabetes, everyone finally agreed that she was uneasy in her new school and was using her accidents as a means to permissibly escape her classroom, and so in came the school behaviorist to help her adjust.

With our disabled kiddos, particularly those who are non/preverbal, we always have to rule out the medical issues first when we witness behavioral changes, since those are often the easiest to measure and the most straightforward to treat. But when we're begging our children to tell us about their day, if it was good or bad, what they did, who they saw, sometimes we can just take note of their intake and output to determine how comfortable they were during their hours away from home.

The kids' travel potty has taken up permanent residence in the trunk of our SUV, which has been helpful in avoiding the sensory nightmare a public restroom can present, from multiple toilets abruptly flushing out of view to hand dryers shutting on and off without any predictable pattern. We keep wipes in the center console of the car. For a while, Hope needed assistance tearing toilet paper from the roll due to her hypotonia, so to increase her independence and privacy in the bathroom, she used pop-up toilet paper that dispenses in a way similar to a tissue box. She continues to wear overnight disposables for stress incontinence, which I see as just really great practice for when we need to think about period underwear during puberty in a couple of years. In the spirit of privacy, she currently uses a visual schedule at school in the nurse's bathroom to remind her of the order of operations when using the toilet (e.g., it's best to wipe after peeing).

With the right people believing in our daughter and imposing no negative bias on her abilities, she is as far as we are concerned a successfully potty trained young lady, who maybe, possibly, perhaps on occasion loses a little when she laughs too hard. Our sweet Hope.

Chapter 15: Working with Others

In addition to using the potty in other places, as explained in detail in Chapter 14, your child is most likely also going to need to learn how to use the potty with other caregivers. Raising a child with disabilities often takes a village, so collaboration is essential while potty training. As I mentioned in Chapter 2, you should always speak to your child's care team before starting potty training. Whether your child is under medical care, goes to daycare or school, attends various therapies, or even just has the occasional babysitter, it is important that everyone stays on the same page throughout the process for clear, consistent messaging.

Also, to prevent your child from developing a preference over who they use the potty with, be sure to have every caregiver involved from as early as possible. If your child is hesitant to use the potty with others, you can gradually ease into that at a pace that makes your child most comfortable. Be sure to offer extra praise for any strides in this area so your child fully understands that everything is okay and they are doing the right thing!

Back to School

Talking to your child's teachers or the school administrators about your potty training plans not only ensures everyone can be on the same page once the diapers are out of the picture, but it also allows for you to learn of any special policies or requirements the school has so those can be taken into account during your potty training process. You may need to have toileting incorporated into your child's IEP (Individualized Education Program) or if allowed, you can make a copy or two of anything you have been documenting to hand out to the classroom teachers, giving them a loose plan to refer back to throughout the day. Having something formal written down will help the teachers and staff provide the best continuity of care. Caregivers should be made aware of things like:

- What do you call the potty? It helps if that vocabulary is the same in all environments. Calling it "potty" at home, but "restroom" at school could lead to confusion.
- Your child's potty signals and cues that they need to go.
- How often they use the bathroom.
- How you handle accidents, including any specific language you prefer to use or avoid.
- How sleep situations are handled if your child naps outside of the home—do they sleep in their underwear or something else?
- How you respond to successes—specific language used and/or rewards.
- Poop schedules.
- Potty preferences (a certain book or video, privacy versus someone in the room, likes to flush versus scared to flush, etc.).
- Sensory needs.

You will also need to provide the caregiver with any necessary supplies, such as:

- Spare changes of clothes.
- Your child's potty or seat insert (if allowed).
- Any rewards or stickers being used.
- A "potty buddy"—a familiar toy from home that your child can take to the bath-room with them when they need to go for added comfort and confidence.
- A family photo—used in similar fashion to the potty buddy.

Also ask if the teachers or aides are willing to, at least loosely, keep track of the times your child uses the bathroom or has accidents, so observations regarding their potty habits and schedule can be made along with any differences between being at home versus being in another environment. Remember that there is going to be a lot of learning and development of skills taking place over the first several weeks of the process, so adjustments might need to be made along the way.

Eventually, you will be sending your child off to school without diapers for the first time and there are a couple of things you can do to help them feel more comfortable using the bathroom in a different setting. First, at drop off, do a little tour of the bathroom your child will be using. If your child has some experience with it already, which they might, have them lead. See if they can show you things like the toilet, the sink, how to turn on the light, those types of things. Be sure you are really playing up how awesome it all seems. You might say, "Whoa, I wish we had foaming soap like that at work! So cool!" or "This little toilet is so cute! It's exactly your size! Can you show me how you sit on it?" If they are able to sit and test out the toilet with you still there, that's a bonus to help them feel more confident once you leave.

Second, have a mini conference between you, your child, and your child's teacher and/or aide to clarify that it's okay for them to ask for help if they need to use the potty while you're away. Get down to your child's eye level and say, "If you need to go potty at school today, just ask Mrs. X and she will help you. Right Mrs. X?" Have the teacher affirm that she is there and happy to help. Sometimes kids can be very shy about asking another grown up about this at first, so if they are certain they can, they'll feel much safer and reassured. If your child is pre- or nonverbal, providing them with a flash card or visual support they can hand to the teacher can take the place of saying the words, "I need to go potty," or they might have "potty" programmed into their AAC device.

Please remember that as your child transitions to school and other environments without diapers for the first time, you might see more accidents. This is very normal, so try to not get discouraged. More often than not, with consistency, your child's success will quickly fall back into place.

When Your Child Won't Use the Potty with Others

Some children are only comfortable using the potty with just mom or just dad when they are first learning. This makes it quite difficult to advance progress when that person has somewhere else they need to be. If your child is struggling to use the potty with a different caregiver, start off with mom or dad in the room with the new caregiver just outside the door, then with them in the room with mom and dad, then with just the new caregiver with mom standing outside the bathroom door, etc. Or have the caregiver help with just one step of the process at first, like washing hands, for example. Baby steps are helpful here—you don't want to push your child too hard, out of risk of regressive or withholding behaviors developing.

It can also be helpful to work with your child more on becoming totally independent with their potty use when possible so they don't need assistance from anyone else during the process. That way they can just take themselves to the potty when they need to go.

Using rewards or offering age-appropriate choices in these instances can also help motivate your child to step outside their comfort zone.

While it may seem daunting to have so many others involved, every person on your child's care team brings perspective and expertise that can tailor the potty training process to your child's specific needs. This collaboration ensures consistency across each different environment, helping your child feel more supported. It also allows for everyone to share effective strategies, as well as the early identification and addressing of any potential issues. By working together as a team, you create a cohesive, compassionate, and comprehensive approach that can improve your overall potty training experience.

Chapter 16: Considerations for Potty Training in an IEP

Potty training our children with disabilities often requires the support of the school environment. Many children with disabilities enter preschool, or sometimes elementary school, while still actively potty training or maybe not yet having fully started. This process often requires additional support and strategies through the child's Individualized Education Program (IEP). Including this information in an IEP helps ensure that children with disabilities receive the personalized assistance they need to achieve success in their toileting routines. The purpose of an IEP is to bridge access to education, and potty training, or "toileting" as the school may refer to it, is a part of the larger story of your child's educational journey.

In this section, we will explore how to effectively incorporate toileting and potty training goals into an IEP. We will cover the necessary components to include, from setting realistic objectives to specifying the supports and accommodations required. By integrating these goals into an IEP, parents and educators can create a structured, comprehensive, and ultimately effective plan that promotes independence, dignity, and success for your child.

With the right strategies and support in place, children with disabilities can make significant progress in their potty training journey, both at home and during their school day.

The Importance of Including Potty Training in an IEP

For children with disabilities, mastering toileting skills is an important milestone that promotes independence and builds self-esteem. While it is very typical of children with disabilities to start their educational career without being fully potty trained, it is not easy to watch your child require this assistance while many of their peers are independently toilet trained. We get it, because we've been there, or are currently there! This is why it is important to come up with a plan that you can feel good about, one that respects your child's dignity and sets them up for success. Including specific potty training goals in your child's IEP helps outline a structured plan that teachers, parents, and support staff can follow consistently across home and school environments.

Developing Effective IEP Potty Training Goals

Setting realistic, measurable goals is the foundation of any effective IEP. Here are sample goals that may help guide the development of toileting skills:

- **Self-advocacy:** "[Child] will indicate, verbally or non-verbally, when they need to be changed or use the restroom." This can be observed and measured through structured observations.
- **Clothing management:** "[Child] will pull up and down their pants when using the restroom." Success can be monitored through regular observations.
- **Personal hygiene:** "[Child] will wipe after using the toilet and wash their hands afterward." Each skill can have individual success rates, tracked through observations.
- **Toileting independence:** "[Child] will use the toilet or urinal appropriately and complete all steps of the process independently." This will be tracked via a potty log shared with parent(s) [weekly/monthly].

These goals should be tailored to your child's abilities and current stage in their potty training journey. By involving both school staff and parents, everyone can ensure your child receives consistent support and guidance.

Accommodations for School-Based Potty Training

A successful potty training plan also requires specific accommodations to meet your child's needs. Here are some possible accommodations to consider:

- *Routine check-ins:* Staff can ask your child regularly if they need to use the re-stroom, especially during high-activity times. It is important to outline any discre-tion you would like staff to use to maintain privacy, especially around older chil-dren.
- *Designated bathroom locations:* Your child might bene-fit from using specific bathrooms within the school, such as a nearby classroom bathroom or the nurse's office, which may be more private or sensory friendly.
- *Supplies and equipment:* You may need to provide items such as training un-derwear, disposable training pants, or extra clothing. Additional tools like step stools and adaptive toilet seats can help support independence. Children with low tone or fine motor delays may benefit from toilet paper dispensers that are easier to grab from.
- *Communication supports:* Visual aids, such as social stories or picture charts, can help remind your child of each toileting step. Communication devices like an Augmentative and Alternative Communication (AAC) device can be pro-grammed to allow your child to communicate their potty needs. Similarly, if your child uses sign language, any staff working with them should be aware of their potty signs.
- *Sensory considerations:* If the bathrooms at school

utilize automatic flushing or hand dryers, consider options for modifications, such as providing paper towels or ways to deactivate automation. (Sticky notes are great for covering flushing sensors!)

- It's essential to approach these accommodations with flexibility and creativity, tailoring them to your child's unique needs, as well as considering the classroom environment.

School and Parent Collaboration

Effective potty training in a school setting also involves open communication between parents and school staff. Schools and parents can create shared routines and strategies, promoting continuity and encouraging your child's progress across environments. Pairing a unique strengths-based approach with the knowledge your child's team has about the school and scheduling will yield the greatest success! Sample Template for Communicating with the School:

Good morning [Case Manager & Teacher],
I am excited to share that we worked really hard on potty training recently and [Child] has made great progress. I wanted to share what is working best so she can have success at school.

- *She does best when we bring her to the potty every 90 mins to 2 hours. She's not always prompting us, or saying yes if we ask her, especially when there is a lot going on. She's great about going if the group or if someone else is going.*
- *Potty before and after [transition to specials such as gym, therapy or rest time].*
- *She's wearing thick training underwear, which fortunately doesn't leak as much. I will send plenty of extra clothing with her.*
- *If she has a poop accident, you have my permission to throw out the dirty un-derwear. It does not need to be cleaned/returned.*

- I will send some disposable training pants in, but I'd prefer if they were used as a last resort. :)

Thank you so much for your partnership here! Please feel free to reach out anytime if we need to tweak anything to work better for [Child] and/or the classroom flow. Please share with any other members of her team.

You can also consider requesting a call with your child's team to talk through any questions or concerns around potty training, so that everyone is on the same page. Communication is the key to success, especially when it comes to potty training.

Understanding State and District Guidelines on Potty Training

Regulations and resources vary by state and district, so it's essential to understand local policies around potty training. Some schools may have accident policies or limitations on the physical assistance staff can provide. Before starting, ask questions, such as:

- **What is your accident policy?** Understanding the school's protocol on accidents can help you plan for various situations.
- **Can you support potty training, and if so, how?** Knowing what assistance is available ensures that you can adjust your home plan accordingly.
- **Is there documentation for potty training progress?** Regular updates from school staff about your child's potty habits can reveal patterns or areas that need attention.

Being proactive in understanding school guidelines and communicating openly with staff can set your child up for success. With the right goals, accommodations, and collaboration, children with disabilities can make meaningful progress in their potty training journey while attending school. The school environment can be a valuable support system, helping your child foster a sense of independence and dignity as they develop their new potty skills.

Conclusion: Embrace Your Version of Success

Potty training, especially for children with disabilities, is a journey that requires patience, persistence, and adaptability. It's a winding path filled with both challenges and triumphs, and every step forward, no matter how small, is a victory worth celebrating! There is no one-size-fits-all method that works for all children, and success stems from a customized plan that considers your child's personality, your family values, and everyone's specific needs. Remember that the process should feel gradual and manageable instead of rushed and stressful, and one of the most important things to consider as you get started is your own readiness and mindset.

This said, potty training doesn't need to fall solely on your shoulders. Don't forget to involve your child's entire care team in the process. Collaboration and open communication among your child's doctors, teachers, and therapists, as well as other members of your family, are crucial. By coordinating efforts and keeping everyone on the same page, the team can help you tailor the potty training process to your child's unique needs, ensuring consistency and supporting their overall comfort and development.

Remember that one of the most important steps of potty training children with disabilities comes well before saying goodbye to diapers. Potty training is a complex, learned skill that requires a gradual and planned approach, so preparing your child and introducing the concept of potty training in advance can make the process go a lot more smoothly. There are plenty of fun ways to make the process engaging and enjoyable for your child without putting pressure on them to abruptly change their routine. This will help build their interest and confidence, while minimizing resistance.

As you are thinking about starting the process, determining the right time to start can greatly impact your success. This timing varies for every family and depends on several factors, including your child's developmental readiness and any other transitions that may be occurring in their life around the same time. Especially for children with disabilities, it's important to focus on developmental signs of readiness rather than age alone, as your child may take longer to reach this stage than their neurotypical peers, which is perfectly okay!

While you're down in the trenches, keep reminding yourself that success isn't just about getting pee or poop in the potty; it is also your child understanding new concepts and getting comfortable with a bathroom routine, learning some key aspects, like releasing on the potty or telling you when they need to go. As frustrating as they can be, accidents are a necessary and important part of the process, and staying calm and patient while focusing on progress will help both you and your child stay positive. Know that resistance, fears, and sensory struggles can be a common part of potty training for children with disabilities, but it doesn't necessarily mean that your child isn't ready or that you've done anything wrong. I've covered some effective strategies to help them overcome these challenges—it might just take some extra patience and understanding on your part.

Another thing I'd like you to take away from this book is that it's important to strike a balance between being prepared and being flexible. Don't let potty training hold you hostage; try to blend it into your routine as much as possible. Just because you've ditched the diapers doesn't mean that you need to be stuck at home, and let's be honest, in today's busy world of parenting, that just isn't realistic, anyway! As I have continued to stress, your child thrives on their routine, so allow them to carry on with it as much as possible, even once you've started potty training.

Potty training children with disabilities is both a challenging and rewarding journey that requires plenty of patience and persistence. But with the right tools, strategies, and preparation, it can start to feel like something manageable, no longer something daunting. Success is born from the determination to keep going, even when the road gets tough, while at the same time knowing when it's okay to give yourselves grace and not push too hard.

Dear Reader,

As our time together comes to an end, your potty training journey is likely just beginning. I fully acknowledge that it's easy to feel overwhelmed or discouraged when progress seems slow or when your experience looks different from others'. Please remember that success and progress have different definitions for every family. In most cases, your child's pace is the right pace, and their progress, however it unfolds, is valid and important. Every challenge you face, every step you take, and every milestone you celebrate will bring you and your child closer to your potty training goals. Although it's all-consuming while you're in it, potty training will eventually be a distant memory, and one I hope you are able to look back on with pride and love.

Speaking of love, your love, confidence, and determination are incredibly powerful tools in this process. Please never forget that you were chosen to be your child's parent for a reason, and deep down, you know what is best for them. Don't let comparisons steal your joy or make you doubt your child's or your own abilities. You are doing an incredible job by supporting and empowering your child with skills they will carry with them for the rest of their lives.

Above all, especially when times get tough, be kind to yourself. This process is hard, and it's not about perfection but about persistence and compassion. Recognize the strength it takes to guide your child through this important part of their development. As you've seen from our Extra Lucky Community Parent Experiences throughout the book, you are not alone in this journey, and the progress you and your child make together is something to be truly proud of.

If at any point you feel like you need additional support, please know that myself and my team are here for you. We are passionate about helping families say goodbye to diapers and making potty training a positive and successful experience. Don't hesitate to reach out if you would like us to work alongside you to meet your goals and help you get the success you and your child deserve.

Happy Pottying! xo
With love,

Allison

Positive Mantras
for Potty Training

by Taryn Lagonigro, Certified Yoga & Meditation Facilitator

Mantras are positive phrases or affirmations that you can say to yourself to find motivation or encouragement. They can be really helpful to change the way you are looking at something or to reset your journey. There are some suggested mantras below. You can also feel free to come up with your own that fit you and your child's journey better; just remember to speak to them in a positive tone ("I am…" instead of "I won't…" for example).

We are moving at the pace we are meant to.

My child is not defined by their toileting habits.

I am doing a great job approaching this journey.

We have both come so far.

Our potty training journey will continue to get easier.

I have the strength to see this through.

I am not alone, I have the support of community.

Meditations for the Potty Training Caregiver

by Taryn Lagonigro, Certified Yoga & Meditation Facilitator

Meditation is often thought of as having to be this unattainable moment of the mind without any chatter. That is not the reality for many of us. Expecting a busy caregiver to sit in total silence without thoughts running through their mind is like expecting potty training to be an entirely linear process. That said, an active meditation is a great way to calm yourself down, quiet your mind (even a little bit!), and keep you grounded during a stressful journey. We hope you enjoy these prompts below. We also love many of the popular meditation apps and free online content as well!

Meditation for Inner Peace & Calm

Sit comfortably in a quiet place. Close your eyes and focus on your breath. With each inhale, imagine breathing in peace and calmness. With each exhale, release any tension or worry you may be carrying. Repeat silently to yourself: "With each breath, I find peace. With each breath, I find calm." Continue this practice for several minutes, allowing yourself to fully immerse in the sensation of tranquility.

Meditation for Self-Compassion

Find a comfortable seated position and place your hand over your heart. Take a few deep breaths, tuning into the rhythm of your heartbeat. As you breathe, repeat the following phrases silently to yourself: "May I be kind to myself. May I be patient with myself. May I be gentle with myself." Allow these words to cultivate a sense of self-compassion and understanding, acknowledging that caregiving can be demanding, but you are doing the best you can.

Meditation for Gratitude

Sit quietly and bring to mind three things you are grateful for in this moment, however small or seemingly insignificant they may seem. With each reflection, allow yourself to fully experience the gratitude and appreciation for these blessings in your life. As you continue this practice, let gratitude fill your heart and uplift your spirit, serving as a reminder of the beauty and abundance that surrounds you even amidst difficulties.

Endnotes

1   *Merriam-Webster Dictionary*, "adaptive," accessed December 17, 2024, https://www.merriam-webster.com/dictionary/adaptive.

2   "Children with Disabilities," UNICEF, updated June 2023, https://data.unicef.org/topic/child-disability.

3   Megan Simon, Sarah Wilkes-Gillan, Yu-Wei Ryan Chen, Reinie Cordier, Alycia Cantrill, Lauren Parsons, Jia Jun Phua, "Toilet Training Interventions for Children with Autism Spectrum Disorder: A Systematic Review," *Research in Autism Spectrum Disorders* 99, (2022): 102049. https://doi.org/10.1016/j.rasd.2022.102049.

4   Taylor Dreher, Kristine Wolter-Warmerdam, Samantha Holland, Terry Katz, Lina Patel, "Toilet Training in Children and Adolescents with Down Syndrome," *Journal of Developmental and Behavioral Pediatrics* 43, no. 6 (2022): e381-e389. https://doi.org/10.1097/DBP.0000000000001058.

5   Mark L. Wolraich and Sherill Tippins, eds., *American Academy of Pediatrics Guide to Toilet Training*. Bantam Books, 2003.

6   Mia E. Lang, "Among Healthy Children, What Toilet-Training Strategy Is Most Effective and Prevents Fewer Adverse Events (Stool Withholding and Dysfunctional Voiding)? Part B: Clinical Commentary," *Pediatrics & Child Health* 13, no. 3 (2008): 203-204. https://doi.org/10.1093/pch/13.3.203.

7   Bruce Taubman, Nathan J. Blume, Nicole Nemeth, "Stool Toileting Refusal: A Prospective Intervention Targeting Parental Behavior," *Archives of Pediatrics and Adolescent Medicine*, 157, no. 12 (2003): 1193-1196. https://doi.org/10.1001/archpedi.157.12.1193.

8   Regine Zopf, Claire Marie Giabbiconi, Thomas Gruber, Matthias M. Müller, "Attentional Modulation of the Human Somatosensory Evoked Potential in a Trial-by-Trial Spatial Cueing and Sustained Spatial Attention Task Measured with High Density 128 Channels EEG," *Cognitive Brain Research* 20, no. 3 (2004): 491-509. https://doi.org/10.1016/j.cogbrainres.2004.02.014.

9   Alan E. Kazdin. "The Kazdin Method for Developing and Changing Behavior of Children and Adolescents," *International Journal of Mental Health Promotion* 23, no. 4 (2021): 429–442. https://doi.org/10.32604/IJMHP.2021.019135.

10 Judy Cameron, Katherine M. Banko, W. David Pierce. "Pervasive Negative Effects of Rewards on Intrinsic Motivation: The Myth Continues," *The Behavior Analyst* 24, no. 1 (2001): 1-44. https://doi.org/10.1007/BF03392017.

11 Patricia Long, Rex Forehand, Michelle Wierson, and Allison Morgan, "Does Parent Training With Young Noncompliant Children Have Long-Term Effects?" *Behaviour Research and Therapy* 32, no. 1 (1994): 101-107. https://doi.org/10.1016/0005-7967(94)90088-4.

12 Tamera L. Wiggins, Kate Sofronoff, and Matthew R. Sanders, "Pathways Triple P–Positive Parenting Program: Effects on Parent-Child Relationships and Child Behavior Problems," *Family Process* 48, no. 4 (2009): 517-30. https://doi.org/10.1111/j.1545-5300.2009.01299.x.

13 Stephen Shei-Dei Yang, Lu-Lu Zhao, Shang-Jen Chang. "Early Initiation of Toilet Training for Urine Was Associated With Early Urinary Continence and Does not Appear to Be Associated With Bladder Dysfunction," *Neurology and Urodynamics* 30, no. 7 (2011): 1253-1257. https://onlinelibrary.wiley.com/doi/10.1002/nau.20982.

14 Summer, Karen. "Toilet Training Children with Down Syndrome." National Down Syndrome Society. Accessed July 10, 2024. https://ndss.org/resources/toilet-training-children-with-down-syndrome.

Acknowledgements

In addition to their families, friends and supportive Potty Training Consultant and Extra Lucky Moms communities, Allison, Taryn & Jess would like to acknowledge the following:

Thank you to our parent contributors Amanda, Carly, Courtney, Elena, Kristi and Megan for your honesty, vulnerability and humor in sharing your potty journeys! We appreciate your willingness to write on such a private topic, knowing that it will help many parents to come.

Thank you to our sponsors Focus Posters, Hyfiber, Jool Baby, Lucky & Me and Squatty Potty. We are grateful you have created products that have made this journey easier for families. By investing in this project, you are showing the world that the disability community matters, and we are so grateful to you for helping us bring this project to life.

Thank you to Kristin Broek, Carley Storm, Lindsay Cook, Annie D'Agostino and our photo shoot models for bringing the various pieces of this book to life visually. Your energy, positivity and creativity made this book as beautiful as it is!

Thank you to Dr Michelle Sirak, Lora Jackle, Brittany Steindl and Sarah Bossio for providing your professional input to this project. Your contributions, and ongoing dedication to the disability community, are so appreciated.

A special thank you to Elena Croy, for providing your keen eye to this book, not only in editing, but with the respect of the disability community in mind. The time you put into this project is something we will never forget. You are an incredible advocate, mother and friend, and we are *extra lucky* to know you.

Bios

Allison Jandu

Allison is a highly sought-after potty training consultant who has guided thousands of families through one of childhood's most significant milestones—potty training. Her expertise spans across children of all ages and abilities. With a focus on fostering independence and empowerment, Allison creates customized potty training plans that lead to lasting success.

As a mother of two, Allison brings both professional expertise and personal experience to her work. She holds a Bachelor of Science degree from the University of Baltimore and has accumulated over 5,000 hours of evidence-based research in potty training, early childhood development, human behavior, and psychology.

Allison has also contributed extensively to the education of childcare professionals and parents by writing internationally accredited training programs and developing a series of acclaimed online courses. Her insights have been featured on platforms such as Good Morning America, New York Magazine, and BuzzFeed. Additionally, Allison is the author of two popular children's books, Let's Go to the Potty! and How Do You Poo?, both available on Amazon. Her expertise has made her a trusted subject matter expert for companies like Little Spoon and Ingenuity, and she generates over 1 million social media impressions each month.

Allison is on a mission to revolutionize the way society approaches potty training, and she thrives on helping children succeed.

Taryn Lagonigro & Jess Quarello
Extra Lucky Moms

The ELM brand was founded in 2021 by Taryn Lagonigro and Jess Quarello to support caregivers in the disability community and educate others on the worth of individuals with disabilities. Now among the largest community of its kind, ELM represents countless common and rare disabilities, with over 50 million social media impressions and growing. In 2024, Taryn and Jess received the National Down Syndrome Congress Media Award and became Little Spoon brand parenting experts, while continuing to be trusted partners for many brands seeking to include the disability community. They co-host the popular Extra Lucky Podcast to elevate voices and nurture caregivers in the disability community. Their book, Dear Mama: Stories of an Extra Lucky Life, has been shared with countless new moms, including through major hospital networks and disability organizations.

Jess and Taryn frequently appear on podcasts, interviews, and at corporate DEI events. Their work has been featured on The Today Show, CBS affiliates, and in countless print publications. With vast personal and professional experience as mothers and leaders, Jess and Taryn are united in their mission to support caregivers and champion the worth of individuals with disabilities.

Four Clovers Publishing

Four Clovers Publishing is a publishing house dedicated to elevating diverse voices and stories. Founded by Taryn Lagonigro, the company is committed to producing books that promote inclusion, representation, and empowerment.

Four Clovers Publishing was established with the mission of amplifying underrepresented narratives and providing authors with the tools and support to share their unique perspectives. With a focus on educational resources, advocacy-driven storytelling, and children's literature, Four Clovers offers books that foster awareness, acceptance, and meaningful conversations.

In addition to publishing, Four Clovers works closely with authors, illustrators, and industry professionals to ensure that each book aligns with its core values of authenticity, accessibility, and impact. The company's commitment to quality storytelling has led to partnerships with advocates, educators, and families, ensuring that every book serves as a resource for learning and understanding.

As a woman-owned and disability-inclusive publishing house, Four Clovers Publishing is shaping the future of literature by ensuring that all stories—especially those that have been historically overlooked—are heard and celebrated.